W9-ANN-655

My Grandmother's Table

My Grandmother's Table

Simple Low-Fat Family Cooking

by her granddaughter
AMY SIMON

GARDNER PUBLISHING

Produced by Tripart, Ltd.
118 East 25th Street
New York, NY 10010

Photography: George G. Wieser
Food Styling: Hilary Snyder
Creative Director: Tony Meisel
Editor: Sarah May Clarkson
Nutritional Analysis: Hedi Levine
Illustrations courtesy Zedcor, Inc., 3420 N. Dodge Blvd., Suite 2, Tucson, AZ 85716

Origination and Printing by Emirates Printing Press

Printed in Dubai, United Arab Emirates

ISBN 0-914373-41-2

Dedication

When I was sixteen, I was blessed with a new grandmother, Mommom Millie. Mommom used to say there was no family problem that couldn't be solved by sitting down at the table to a good meal. Alas, this experience has become rare in our fast-paced lives. Mommom taught me how to cook with love and joy. Every recipe I have created or made my own has been developed by using the principles of cooking as I learned them from her. This book, which includes many of her original recipes reworked into low-fat form, is dedicated to her, my inspiration, my friend. I hope they have a beautiful kitchen in heaven where she can play.

Menu

Special Thanks

I would like to thank my husband, Joe Gardner, first and foremost for making this book possible. He not only serves as its publisher but it was at his suggestion that I have written it. I appreciate his confidence in me as an author, and I bask in the adoration of his discerning palate. Thank you to my daughter, Hannah Rose, who generously shared much of her first year of life with her adopted sibling, this cook book.

Thank you to the rest of my family for their support, notably my stepmother Rosemarie Simon for bringing her mother into my life, and my mother Beverly Werner for her encouraging words. Thanks to Barb and Jim McNichol for digging through tons of boxes to locate a picture of the camera shy Mommom Millie, and my cousin Rob for his computer support. Thanks to my Mothers Group for taste testing my new recipes every Friday and to my dearest friend Nancy Hamada, who bravely helped me edit down the recipes to fit in this book. For me it was like casting pearls out to sea.

Before You Begin

So much talk about low-fat food these days. What's a regular person like me to do? My family has their favorite meals, food that they will eat, and that's that. I've tried to make changes before, but the low fat food tastes so awful, they won't eat it, and, frankly, I don't like it either! Sound familiar? It is difficult these days to prepare food while negotiating all the new information and new products that we are constantly bombarded with. There are so many products on the market that are supposed to make eating a low-fat diet easier, but it just seems to make shopping for food a lot more difficult and time consuming.

Don't despair!

In this book, I try to help you find your way around these products and eating ideas so you can still have the familiar foods you and your family love. We need to learn how to use the low-fat foods available to their best advantage. For example, nonfat sour cream does not taste like its full-fat counterpart. But, with a few spices here and a dab of low-fat mayonnaise there, you can make it pass with ease. Once you're familiar with the recipes in this book, you will have learned techniques that you can use to make your own recipes low-fat and delicious.

Before you begin, you should know a little bit about my cooking philosophy. I'm a big fan of the "never-say-diet" diet. I enjoy hearty portions of food, including desserts. I don't count calories closely, but I do watch fat grams, and I believe exercise is essential for physical and mental health. I am responsible for the nutritional needs of my family, and I follow these guidelines to keep them healthy and happy. My goal for this book is to show you how to prepare healthy, low-fat, familiar dishes, and to give you some new cooking ideas that the whole family will love.

The minute I hear the word diet, I think of restrictions, things I can never eat again. 'Diet' makes my husband cranky, and my family resentful, anticipating a menu of bland and unexciting foods, and a frustrated and depressed mommy. I realized that I had to change the whole way I looked at food and weight. I needed to change the way we ate by developing low-fat recipes for my family's favorite foods. In doing so, we could eat more healthily, without neglecting our cravings—if we learned to eat food low in fat as a general rule, we could splurge on occasion (although who needs to when we have my low-fat desserts!), and still maintain a healthy weight, a lower cholesterol level, and a guiltless state of mind.

Peace of mind is the most important aspect of healthy eating.

We spend so much time thinking about what we want to eat, feeling guilty about what we have already eaten, and dieting and bingeing. This is a negative cycle to get caught up in, and a bad example to set for our children.

I do not write about how to diet in these pages— I write about a way to eat. I show you how to increase your food options, not diminish them. My recipes do not obsess about calories (although you should keep them in mind—a low-fat, high-calorie diet will cause you to gain undesired weight, too).

It's important that you clearly recognize fat. These recipes have all of the flavor, but less of the fat, of their traditional counterparts. So whether you want your family to lose weight, or you simply want them to eat healthier, these recipes are for you. Feeding your family can be a quick, easy and healthy experience that brings you together, creating a time in your day to spend reconnecting with each other.

So, whether you're a mom who works and is still responsible for the shopping, cooking and feeding of your family, or you're a dad or significant other with these same responsibilities, this book will help you prepare delicious, wholesome, low-fat, home-cooked favorites that will make your family want to join you at the table.

Let's talk about fat.

The current standard for a healthy, low-fat diet, according to the American Medical Association, is that no more than 30 percent of your daily calories should come from fat (some physicians believe that your fat consumption should be no more than 25 percent of daily totals). All of the food products in your super-market are now required to have labels that include the fat content per serving. Learn to read those labels.

Some nutritional experts say that the easiest way to achieve the 30 percent goal is to never eat anything that has higher than 30 percent fat content. This means if a product has 100 calories and 31 or more come from fat, you can't have it. Now, I don't like anyone to tell me I can't have something—it just makes me want it more. I find a more successful approach is to figure out how many fat grams you can have a day for the weight you are (to maintain your weight), or want to be (to lose weight). Then choose your food to fit into the daily totals.

Below is an equation that I have found successful for figuring out optimum daily fat grams. It's based on a chart in *The 8-Week Cholesterol Cure* by Robert Kowalski (Harper Collins). If you decide you want an extra 10 grams of fat as a treat at dinner, you can eliminate those grams from some other meal (have a low-fat dressing on your salad at lunch). Save up your fat grams!

I find this method empowering, and it gives me more food options to choose from.

You can use this concept to plan your weekly menu. Say your birthday is coming up, and you plan on having a big piece of cake. Plan in advance by restricting your fat grams before the day.

Figuring Your Daily Fat Grams

Multiply:
Your optimal weight in pounds by
the number of calories per pound if you are:

Male who exercises moderately—15 calories per pound
Male who doesn't exercise—13 calories per pound
Female who exercises moderately—13 calories per pound
Female who doesn't exercise—10 calories per pound

I am 110 pounds, times 13 calories means 1,430 calories per day. Then, I will divide total daily calories by the percentage of fat I have chosen to eat—25 percent of 1,430 calories is 357.50 calories from fat per day. There are nine calories in each gram of fat, so I divide my daily fat calorie total by 9 to get the number of fat grams I can have in a day, which totals approximately 40 grams.

Now, about exercise.

Exercise is essential for a healthy body and imperative for a healthy mind. It also makes you feel better. Getting your heart rate up through exercise releases a chemical called endorphins in your body, which works like a "feel good" pill. Exercise tones your body and makes it stronger. Exercise helps your body work more efficiently—your heart works better, sweating releases toxins from your system, and you can burn calories more efficiently. The last point is the most important one for me—I can eat more and not gain weight. It's a great concept because I, like a number of people I know, "live to eat" instead of "eat to live."

I've heard complaints from people trying to lose weight that when they exercise, they want to eat more. It's true, that can happen, especially at first. It's not a problem, you can eat all you feel you need—just choose a recipe from this book. Eventually, exercise will suppress your hunger—the endorphins will be food enough for your body. Don't forget to make sure the whole family gets involved, too.

This doesn't mean to go without food. Never skip a meal. Put some kind of food into your system at least six times a day. It could be as little as a carrot or a piece of fruit. You don't want to paralyze your metabolism by starving it. The minute you tell your body it is starving, the metabolism slows down so that you burn calories more slowly. It's a natural defense mechanism that nature gives us so that during times of famine, we can survive on less food. It also means that fat will stay on your body longer, so avoid this. Carry little snacks with you, or keep them at your desk at work. Encourage your family to do the same.

Learn to recognize when you are full. It takes the brain twenty minutes to get the signal from your stomach that you've had enough to eat. We must learn to take at least twenty minutes to eat our meal.

I have found this to be one of the hardest changes in my life. As a breast feeding Mom, I'm not only ravenous when I sit down at the table, but I'm always rushing to attend to my baby—I'm either afraid that her cooperative mood won't last long enough for me to eat, or that she'll interrupt the dining experience for the rest of the family. Well, I had to get over that. I purposefully make myself eat more slowly every time I face my plate, especially at dinner when I have help from her father. If my daughter gets fussy at mealtime, we take turns engaging her while the other eats, allowing us all the time we need. Okay, I admit that circumstances don't always afford us this luxury, but when it does, we know how to take advantage of it.

So, before you take that second helping (which you can do if your daily totals allow it), wait twenty minutes from your first bite, and reassess if you really are still hungry. It may only be a sweet that you need to assuage that desire. It is said that a sweet after a meal will tell your brain that the meal is finished, and will slow down your hunger.

What's the story on sugar?

A lot of people use a sugar substitute to save on calories—I don't. We have all heard of the dangers of saccharin. We know less about the long-term affects of other sugar substitutes, like Aspartame. I was told by my health care professional not to consume it while I was pregnant, so that was enough of a concern for me.

You should know that sugar is a very powerful food additive. It is a stimulant, and has been found to be addicting. Sugar also turns to fat in the system. So, consumption of sugar should be watched closely, especially refined sugars (e. g. white sugar). A lot of hidden sugars can be found in processed foods. Read the labels.

Some other sugars are fructose—a natural sugar found in fruit—honey, maple syrup, malt syrups, etc. They are all high in calories, so watch that you don't overdo it on the sweets. But if you feel the desire to have something sinful, the recipes in this book are a good way to go. I'm not one to advocate giving up sugar—I like it too much, and it's integral to my emotional well-being. My low-fat dessert recipes almost all have some kind of sugar in them, although there is less than in their full-fat counterparts, and my portions are a nice size—no slivers here! Eat them wisely. Balance in your diet is the key, depriving yourself of nothing, but making healthier choices on the whole. You may not be able to keep the kids from wanting McDonalds, but you can reduce the number of trips to the fast food chains by having tasty food choices at home.

That is the purpose of this book—to empower you to easily feed yourself and your family a variety of family favorites, of all kinds, and to live a healthier lifestyle. I have found it works best if you can do most of your cooking at home, where you can control the amount of fat in your food (not to mention the benefits to your pocket book!). Frankly, you don't even need to tell your loved ones that they are eating low-fat food. Save the anarchy, and let them think their favorite dishes have been prepared the same way as they always have, with just a spice or two added.

Cooking, unlike baking, is an art, not a science. It is interpretive—each cook must put his or her own stamp on a recipe, appealing to their individual taste. That's why I have included a 'Notes' column with every recipe. I encourage you, I implore you, to make notes on what you like, or would like to change, about these recipes. Make it your own. In the dessert section, you'll need to stick closely to the original recipe, although flavorings can be substituted.

How To Read These Recipes

Each recipe is in an easy-to-read format.

I try to write as if my sister Lauren, "the doctor," is reading the recipe—she can remove a bullet from a man's brain, but she can't boil water!

First comes the title of the recipe—I use the traditional name, but the dish will always be low-fat.

Next to the title is a "time circle" with two times in it—*Prep* and *Cook*. The prep time is the amount of time it takes to get all of your ingredients ready to use. This time can also include precooking of ingredients. I encourage you to always prepare your ingredients before you begin to cook, so you have everything you need at your finger tips, and can pay better attention to the dish developing, instead of leaving it unattended while you chop or dice something. I have figured the Prep Time based on how long it takes me—time will vary according to your experience in the kitchen.

The lower half of the time circle is the cook time. This is the time it takes to cook or bake the dish. These symbols should tell you immediately if you have the time it will take to prepare the recipe, or if you should choose another one.

Next is the photograph of the dish, ready to devour. This photo will help you see how the dish can look when it's completed, but your results will not necessarily look the same. Be creative, do your own thing—my picture is just a guide.

Next, the Ingredients are listed, including how each should be prepared. Each will be portioned by number needed, approximate size, and by weight, spoon or cup size. I use the measurements that you would find most readily at the store—for example, if I ask you to use cream cheese, I would list it by ounces instead of cups, since the block of cheese you would purchase would be measured in ounces. Yet, while cheddar cheese may be measured in ounces in the store, if the recipe calls for grated cheese, I will measure it in cups.

If you have any doubts about the amount of an ingredient, don't despair. In cooking, unlike baking, most ingredients can be altered according to taste. Do your best, keep notes, and perhaps try it differently next time.

I have also listed the equipment you will need with each recipe, to help you know whether or not you can accomplish the recipe with the equipment you have. Things like cutting boards and plates are generally omitted.

I have then listed step-by-step instructions for preparing the dish. Each step will be headed by the number of minutes it may take you.

Following the step-by-step instructions is a full nutritional analysis for determining how the dish fits into your daily diet.

You will also find some personal notes of mine about each recipe scattered on the pages, including ideas for different ways of preparing the dish.

Finally, there is the note column on the right side of each recipe spread for your personal thoughts.

I have included a Pantry List for easy reference. There are so many choices and options available at the supermarket today to help make low-fat cooking easier and tastier. Substitute dairy products made from lower and nonfat ingredients carry traditional creamy and cheesy flavors with a lot less of the fat. Low-fat margarine and unsweetened fruit sauces make baking and dessert making as desirous as their high-fat, high-calorie counterparts. The Pantry List should help you always have the needed ingredients handy to prepare any recipe from this book.

The key to successfully feeding your family low-fat, delicious food quickly without spending a fortune on frozen entrees, processed food packages, and take-out menus is a little *advanced planning*. This advanced planning includes learning the basics of low-fat substitutions, having a well-stocked pantry, using the proper kitchen tools and preparing some foods in advance and in bulk. Check out the Helpful Hints that can make food preparation and using this book easier and more rewarding.

Enjoy your low-fat eating experience, and have fun!

Pantry List

__extensive variety of dried spices

__olive oil spray

__buttered-flavored spray

__butter-flavored flakes

__egg substitute

__unbleached white flour

__freeze-dried potato flakes

__cornstarch

__nonfat cream cheese

__reduced-fat cheeses

__nonfat mozzarella cheese

__fat-free tomato sauce

__canned crushed tomatoes

__canned whole plum tomatoes

__fresh garlic

__fresh and/or frozen vegetables

__canned beans

__dried beans

__low-fat mayonnaise

__low-fat tub margarine

__low-fat stick margarine (baking only)

__rice, assorted

__canned skimmed evaporated milk

__low-fat pastas

__lemons

__lean turkey products
     sausage, ground meat, fillets, bacon

__chicken breasts

__leanest ground beef

__grated hard cheese,
     Parmesan, Romano

__stocks, canned or frozen,
     nonfat and/or low-sodium
     chicken, beef, vegetable

__frozen spinach

__phyllo dough

__low-fat buttermilk, liquid or powder

__Dijon mustard

__low-fat or nonfat yogurt

__spring or filtered water

__extra virgin olive oil

__red wine vinegar

__balsamic vinegar

__dehydrated salt-free seasoning flakes

Helpful Hints

Prepare food in advance!

Get a deep freezer for storage of meats, bread, sauces and prepared food. This way you'll always have something to serve at your fingertips.

Buy meat, and chicken, in bulk and divide into family size or double portions and freeze. This will save you money and shopping time.

Date everything you freeze or store in the refrigerator.

When storing chicken or meat in the freezer for quick use, pound it thin or butterfly it before freezing.

Buy whole chickens or meat on the bone and cut it up before freezing. Then you'll have bones or necks, backs and skin with which to make homemade stock at no extra cost.

Keep the pantry stocked with the items most often used.

Always have pasta on hand.

When cooking, prepare twice as much and freeze half.

Roast a chicken and refrigerate for a quick cold supper or sandwiches all week.

Make a big pot of tomato sauce each month and freeze it in 2-3 cup servings for pasta, or any Italian dish, in a flash.

When cooking with less fat, use lots of spices, fruit juices and vegetables for more robust flavor.

When eating high fat spreads, cheese or butter on crackers or bread, spread it thinly and eat it spread side down so it touches the taste buds first. You'll get an explosion of flavor for much less of the fat.

When sautéing garlic, onions or other vegetables, add a tablespoon or two of chicken stock instead of oil.

If you are watching your cholesterol levels closely, bake with vegetable oil in liquid form (no more than ¼ cup) instead of the reduced calorie margarine. Hardened fats such as stick margarine should be considered saturated fats.

Always lay out all of your ingredients first so cooking is quicker and less harried and mistakes can be avoided.

Cook with a good set of non-stick cookware to reduce the amount of lubricant, which often means fat, you need to keep food from sticking.

Keep notes (use the note columns in this book) on your cooking experiences and recipes so you don't make the same mistake twice and you won't have to recall from scratch meals that were successful.

Baked Ziti Casserole

Serves 6

Prep 15 min

Cook 60 min

Ingredients
1 lb (455 g) ziti
olive oil spray
1 small onion, diced
½ cup (120 ml) mushrooms, sliced
2 cloves garlic, minced
1 cup low-fat or nonfat ricotta cheese
½ teaspoon (3 ml) parsley
2 tablespoons Parmesan cheese, grated
1½ cups (355 ml) nonfat pasta sauce, jar or homemade
salt and pepper to taste
¾ cup (180 ml) nonfat mozzarella, grated
¼ cup (60 ml) skim milk mozzarella, grated

Equipment
9 x 12-inch casserole
large pot
colander
grater
medium frying pan
measuring cup and spoons

This dish pleases even the pickiest eater.

16

15 minutes	Fill pot halfway with water and bring to a boil. Preheat oven to 400 degrees (205°C).
	Prepare ingredients as listed.
10 minutes	Cook ziti until al dente (pasta should be very chewy).
	Drain in colander. Fill pot with cool water and return pasta to pot.
10 minutes	Spray frying pan with olive oil spray. Over medium heat, sauté onions until translucent. Add mushrooms and sauté until tender. Add garlic, continue to sauté for another few minutes. Do not burn garlic. Remove from heat and set aside.
1 minute	In a bowl, mix ricotta, parsley and Parmesan cheese together.
2 minutes	Drain pasta again and put in large bowl. Mix in vegetables and pasta sauce. Season to taste.
2 minutes	Transfer to casserole dish. Spread ricotta mixture on top, then sprinkle with mozzarella cheese.
35 minutes	Bake for 35 minutes at 400 degrees (205°C).

Approximate nutritional analysis per serving:
Calories 403, Protein 22 g, Carbohydrates 63 g, Fat 6 g,
Saturated Fat 3 g, Cholesterol 20 mg, Sodium 127 mg

Use your favorite vegetables to create a unique dish.

Beef Stew

Serves 6

Ingredients

olive oil spray
3 tablespoons (45 ml) unbleached white flour
salt and pepper
1 lb (455 g) extra-lean beef, cubed into 1-oz pieces
    with all fat trimmed
1 large onion, cubed
5 cloves garlic, sliced
2 large carrots, sliced
1 medium yellow squash, cubed
10 mushrooms, halved
1 small red pepper, seeded and cubed
1 can low-sodium beef broth, defatted
2 bay leaves

1 teaspoon (5 ml) oregano
1 teaspoon (5 ml) dill
1 teaspoon (5 ml) parsley
1 oz (30 ml) dry red wine
3 medium potatoes, cubed

Equipment

cast-iron pot with lid (Dutch oven)
knife
measuring cup and spoons
plastic bag
plate
tongs or fork

Serve with hot reduced-fat biscuits. Delicious on a cold winter's eve!

18

20 minutes   Prepare all ingredients as listed.

Heat cast-iron pot over medium heat. Spray liberally with olive oil spray.

10 minutes   Put flour and some salt and pepper into the plastic bag and add beef cubes. Shake until beef is well coated. Brown beef in warmed pot on all sides and set aside on plate.

3 minutes   Spray pan with olive oil again and sauté onions until translucent. Add garlic, sauté another minute.

1 hour 32 minutes   Add all other vegetables except potatoes to the pan and sauté for 2 minutes. Add beef broth, spices and wine. Return meat to pan. Stir and cover pot. Bring to boil. Reduce heat. Simmer 1½ hours, stirring occasionally so it doesn't stick.

30 minutes   Add potatoes and continue to simmer for 30 minutes or until potatoes are tender. If you want a thicker broth, add some dehydrated potato flakes and stir.

For a meatless stew, add firm tofu chunks, or sweet potatoes, green pepper and/or zucchini with vegetable broth instead.

Approximate nutritional analysis per serving:
Calories 257, Protein 25 g, Carbohydrates 29 g, Fat 8 g,
Saturated Fat 3 g, Cholesterol 53 mg, Sodium 47 mg

Beef stew freezes well; make double and save half for another day.

19

Chicken Pot Pie

Serves 8

Ingredients

2 lbs (910 g) skinned and cubed white-meat chicken
3 cloves garlic, sliced
8 oz (240 g) mushrooms, sliced
1 small green pepper, cleaned and diced
2 large carrots, sliced
2 large white potatoes, cubed
½ cup peas, fresh or frozen
1 large white onion, cubed
½ teaspoon (3 ml) paprika
1 teaspoon (5 ml) parsley
½ teaspoon (3 ml) salt
½ teaspoon (3 ml) pepper
8 oz (240 ml) low-sodium chicken stock, defatted
¼ cup (60 ml) dry white wine

¼ cup (60 ml) dehydrated potato flakes
¾ single pie crust, store bought
    (or low-fat homemade, see Sour Apple Pie recipe)

Equipment

deep casserole dish or 8 ramekins
small saucepan
a sharp knife
measuring cup and spoons

Make this pie in a disposable pie tin and freeze for serving anytime.

20 minutes	Prepare ingredients as listed.
3 minutes	Mix chicken, vegetables and spices together in a bowl and transfer into the casserole dish or ramekins.
5 minutes	In saucepan thicken chicken broth and wine with potato flakes over medium heat. Add more potato flakes if not thick enough; it should be the consistency of gravy.
	Pour liquid over chicken.
5 minutes	Cut out ¼ piecrust and discard. Roll out remaining dough and lay over casserole. Poke holes in top with a fork.
45 minutes	Bake at 350 degrees (180°C) for 45 minutes until crust is lightly brown and vegetables are tender.

Approximate nutritional analysis per serving:
Calories 381, Protein 35 g, Carbohydrates 22 g, Fat 6 g,
Saturated Fat 4 g, Cholesterol 100 mg, Sodium 265 mg

You can make beef pie with extra-lean beef and defatted beef broth or a vegetable pie with vegetable broth and white wine.

Chicken Cacciatore

Serves 10

This recipe makes lots. Freeze some for later!

Ingredients

4 lb (1.8 kg) whole chicken, cut up and skinned, wings removed
¼ cup (60 ml) unbleached white flour
salt and pepper to taste
olive oil spray
1 large white onion, chopped
¼ cup (60 ml) low-sodium chicken broth, defatted
¼ cup (60 ml) dry red wine
5 cloves garlic, sliced
1 small chili pepper, seeded and minced
4 oz (120 g) tomato paste
14 oz (420 g) can peeled plum tomatoes
1 medium yellow squash, cubed
1 medium zucchini, cubed
1 medium red pepper, seeded and sliced

1 medium green pepper, seeded and sliced
2 large carrots, sliced
8 oz (240 g) mushrooms, halved or quartered
½ cup (120 ml) broccoli tops
1 teaspoon (5 ml) oregano
1 teaspoon (5 ml) parsley
½ teaspoon (3 ml) tarragon
2 whole bay leaves

Equipment

Dutch oven with lid
medium mixing bowl
knife
measuring cup and spoons
tongs
plastic bag
plate

Remember that dark meat contains more fat.

22

30 minutes   Prepare ingredients as listed. Divide the chicken breast and legs into two pieces each.

3 minutes   Put the flour and some salt and pepper into a plastic bag. Add the chicken and lightly flour on all sides.

10 minutes   Heat the Dutch oven over medium heat. Spray liberally with olive oil spray. Brown the chicken on all sides and set aside.

6 minutes   Respray the pan and sauté the onions until translucent, adding ½ of the chicken broth to moisten. Add the garlic and chili pepper and sauté another minute, then add the tomato paste, sautéing until it takes on a light color (3 minutes).

5 minutes   Add the canned tomatoes, the rest of the chicken broth if there is any, the wine and the rest of the vegetables and spices. Bring to a boil.

1 hour   Lay the chicken pieces side by side in the pot. Reduce heat to a simmer, cover and cook 1 hour, stirring occasionally and lifting the chicken so it doesn't stick.

Remove the bay leaves before serving.

Approximate nutritional analysis per serving:
Calories 390, Protein 70 g, Carbohydrates 18 g, Fat 9 g,
Saturated Fat 3 g, Cholesterol 202 mg, Sodium 200 mg

Save the skin, neck and back of the chicken to make stock.

Chili

Serves 8

Ingredients

olive oil spray
1½ lbs (685 g) 99 percent lean ground turkey
½ lb (230 g) 90 percent extra-lean ground beef
1 medium onion, finely diced
5 cloves garlic, minced
1 small chili pepper, seeded and minced
4 oz (120 g) tomato paste
14 oz can (420 g) crushed tomatoes
8 oz (240 ml) beer (or nonalcoholic beer)
1 teaspoon (5 ml) salt
1 teaspoon (5 ml) pepper
1 teaspoon (5 ml) cumin
1 tablespoon (15 ml) chili powder
1 teaspoon (5 ml) Tabasco sauce

1 tablespoon (15 ml) parsley
1 teaspoon (5 ml) oregano
1 teaspoon (5 ml) cilantro
1 bay leaf
10-oz can (300 g) red kidney beans, optional

Equipment

cast-iron pot with lid (Dutch oven)
knife
measuring cup and spoons
can opener
fork

This chili freezes well. Store in single servings for quick microwave lunches and dinners.

24

12 minutes   Heat Dutch oven over medium heat. Spray liberally with olive oil spray. Sauté the ground meats using a fork to break it up into fine granules. When cooked through, remove from pot and drain any residual fat. Set aside.

5 minutes   Respray pot with olive oil spray and sauté the onion until almost translucent. Add the garlic and chili pepper and sauté another minute to release their flavors. Add the tomato paste and stir while it cooks for 2 more minutes until the paste appears lighter in color.

1 hour
35 minutes   Add crushed tomatoes, cooked ground meat, beer and spices to the pot. Blend well. Bring to a boil, reduce heat, simmer 1½ hours, stirring occasionally. Do not let liquid evaporate. If it does, add some water and reduce heat.

30 minutes   Add the kidney beans, if desired, simmer for 30 more minutes, and serve.

Serve topped with reduced fat cheddar cheese, a dollop of reduced fat sour cream and some sliced jalapenos and you've got one of my favorite meals!

Approximate nutritional analysis per serving:
Calories 285, Protein 29 g, Carbohydrates 8 g, Fat 6 g,
Saturated Fat 3 g, Cholesterol 67 mg, Sodium 328 mg

Use all turkey meat for even less fat.

Great as a dip for baked tortilla chips.

Macaroni and Cheese

Serves 6

My daughter's favorite!

Ingredients

1 lb (455 g) elbow macaroni
1½ cups (355 ml) evaporated skim milk
½ cup (120 ml) 1 percent milk
2 cups (480 ml) nonfat cheddar cheese
2 oz (60 g) sharp cheddar cheese
8 oz (240 g) nonfat cream cheese
2 tablespoons (30 ml) Parmesan cheese
1 ½ teaspoons (8 ml) Dijon mustard
¼ cup (60 ml) plain bread crumbs
1 teaspoon (5 ml) garlic powder
salt and pepper to taste
butter–flavored oil spray

Equipment

medium pot
8-cup casserole dish
large mixing bowl
cheese grater or food processor
measuring cups and spoons
large spoon
colander

Add broccoli or mushrooms to this casserole for added flavor and nutrition!

Preheat oven to 350 degrees (180°C).

15 minutes Bring water to a boil and cook elbow pasta until al dente and drain liquid in a colander. Set aside in a mixing bowl.

Pour the evaporated skim milk and the low-fat milk into the saucepan and bring to a boil. Lower heat to simmer.

15 minutes Add the cream cheese to the milk and melt. Slowly add the cheddar cheeses and the parmesan cheese to the mixture and stir until melted.

5 minutes Add the garlic powder, salt, pepper and mustard. Stir until ingredients are blended and thick.

5 minutes Pour cheese mixture over the cooked pasta and incorporate.

Spray baking dish with butter flavored oil spray.

Pour mixture into the baking dish.

Top with bread crumbs and spray lightly with butter spray.

10 minutes Broil for 10 minutes or until top is brown and bubbly.

Approximate nutritional analysis per serving:
Calories 209, Protein 26 g, Carbohydrates 14 g, Fat 4 g,
Saturated Fat 3 g, Cholesterol 21 mg, Sodium 486 mg

This cheese sauce is great on just about anything.

Meat Loaf

Serves 6

Prep
15 min

Cook
57 min

Ingredients

1 cup (240 ml) Italian bread crumbs
½ cup (120 ml) low-fat milk
½ lb (230 g) 99 percent lean ground turkey
½ lb (230 g) 90 percent extra-lean ground beef
½ cup (120 ml) egg substitute (or 3 large egg whites)
4 oz (120 g) tomato paste
1 small onion, minced
3 cloves garlic, minced
1 tablespoon (15 ml) dried parsley
dash Worcestershire sauce
salt and pepper, to taste
pinch red pepper flakes
2 tablespoons (30 ml) Parmesan cheese, grated
olive oil spray

Equipment

large bowl
small bowl
measuring cup and spoons
can opener
knife
loaf pan (medium)

You may use all turkey instead of beef.

28

Preheat oven to 400 degrees (205°C).

15 minutes Prepare ingredients as listed.

5 minutes In a small bowl, soak bread crumbs in milk.

5 minutes In large bowl, place all ingredients. Using your hands, knead ingredients together very well.

2 minutes Spray loaf pan with olive oil spray. Pat meat mixture into pan.

Bake 45 minutes.

Approximate nutritional analysis per serving:
Calories 250, Protein 10 g, Carbohydrates 25 g, Fat 5 g,
Saturated Fat 2 g, Cholesterol 18 mg, Sodium 380 mg

Serve with mashed potatoes: whip boiled potatoes with low-fat milk, butter flakes and salt using a hand mixer. Yummy!

Makes great sandwiches.

Meatballs

Makes approximately 40 meatballs

Prep 14 min

Cook 20 min

Ingredients

1½ lbs (685 g) 99 percent lean ground turkey
1¼ cups (295 ml) plain bread crumbs
½–¾ cup (120–180 ml) skim milk
¾ lb (455 g) 90 percent extra–lean ground beef
2 tablespoons (30 ml) Parmesan cheese
I cup (240 ml) egg substitute
1 teaspoon (5 ml) oregano
1 teaspoon (5 ml) parsley
½ teaspoon (3 ml) garlic powder
1 teaspoon (5 ml) salt
½ teaspoon (3 ml) pepper
olive oil spray

Equipment

large mixing bowl
small mixing bowl
large nonstick frying pan
measuring cup and spoons
knife
food processor, optional
tongs

These freeze well. Add them frozen to your favorite sauce for a meal in 15 minutes.

5 minutes	In a food processor, or with a sharp knife, cut up the ground turkey until the meat is very fine.
1 minute	In the small mixing bowl, wet breadcrumbs with milk until moist but not soaked.
3 minutes	In a large mixing bowl, combine ground turkey and ground beef. Using your hands, blend it together well. Mix in soaked bread crumbs, cheese, egg substitute and spices. Mix well.
5 minutes	Using a tablespoon, scoop a heaping portion of the mixture and roll into balls. Set aside.
5 minutes	Spray pan liberally with olive oil spray. Over medium heat, brown meatballs on all sides.
15 minutes	Reduce heat and cook through or add to tomato sauce, if desired, and cook until done.

Approximate nutritional analysis per meatball:
Calories 81, Protein 7 g, Carbohydrates 2 g, Fat <1 g,
Saturated Fat <1 g, Cholesterol 8 mg, Sodium 94 mg

Wet your hands with water to roll out smoother meatballs.

Serve on pasta or make a delicious hero sandwich!

Shepherd's Pie

Serves 6

Ingredients

6 medium potatoes (or organic dried potato flakes)
1 cup (240 ml) low-fat milk
olive oil spray
¾ lb (455 g) 99 percent lean ground turkey
¾ lb (455 g) 90 percent extra lean ground beef
1 small red pepper, seeded and diced
1 large onion, diced
3 cloves garlic, minced
1 cup (240 ml) peas, fresh or frozen
1 cup (240 ml) carrots, fresh (blanched) or frozen, diced
1 tablespoon (15 ml) parsley
salt and pepper to taste
1 teaspoon (5 ml) Worcestershire sauce

½ cup (120 ml) low-sodium beef broth,
    canned or homemade, defatted
1 teaspoon (5 ml) paprika

Equipment

large pot
Dutch oven with lid (cast-iron pot)
colander
large bowl
measuring cup and spoons
peeler
hand mixer
medium bowl

Anything with mashed potatoes makes my family happy!

15 minutes	Bring a pot of water to boil for the potatoes.
	Prepare ingredients as listed. Preheat oven to 350 degrees (180°C).
15-20 minutes	Peel the potatoes and quarter them. Boil until tender.
5 minutes	Drain the potatoes and use a hand mixer to whip them as you slowly pour in the milk. Mix until smooth and fluffy. (Don't overbeat.) Set aside.
10 minutes	Spray the Dutch oven liberally with olive oil spray. Over medium heat sauté the meat using a fork to separate into fine kernels. Drain off the excess grease. Set aside.
5 minutes	Spray the pot again with olive oil spray. Sauté the peppers, onions and garlic. Add the peas, carrots, spices and Worcestershire sauce.
3 minutes	Return the meat to the pot, add beef broth and salt and pepper to taste. Bring to a boil.
2 minutes	Turn off the heat. Spread the mashed potatoes over the top of the meat. Sprinkle with paprika.
30 minutes	Bake without lid at 350 degrees (180°C) until potatoes are golden brown.

Approximate nutritional analysis per serving:
Calories 466, Protein 34 g, Carbohydrates 39 g, Fat 4.5 g,
Saturated Fat 2 g, Cholesterol 55 mg, Sodium 90 mg

You may use all ground turkey for a leaner dish.

Sloppy Joes

Serves 6

Ingredients

olive oil spray
1½ lbs (685 g) 99 percent lean ground turkey breast
1 medium onion, diced
1 small green pepper, seeded and diced
1 small red pepper, seeded and diced
4 cloves garlic, minced
5 plum tomatoes, seeded
6-oz can (180 g) tomato paste
½ teaspoon (3 ml) oregano
½ teaspoon (3 ml) parsley
¼ teaspoon (1 ml) crushed red pepper, optional
½ cup (120 ml) spring water
6 low-fat hamburger buns

Equipment

Dutch oven (cast-iron pot)
colander
knife
measuring cup and spoons
large spoon, can opener

I learned this recipe as a Girl Scout a long, long time ago.

34

15 minutes	Prepare ingredients as listed.
	Spray pot liberally with olive oil spray.
10 minutes	Over medium heat, sauté ground turkey well, breaking it down to small morsels with a fork. When thoroughly cooked, drain any grease and set aside.
7 minutes	Spray pot again with olive oil spray. Sauté onions and peppers until onions are almost translucent. Add garlic and tomatoes. Sauté another 2 minutes.
2 minutes	Add the tomato paste, sauté until lighter in color.
2 minutes	Return the turkey to the pot. Add spices and water. Mix well.
20 minutes	Let simmer, covered, for 20 minutes or longer, if desired.
	Serve over fresh warmed hamburger buns.

Approximate nutritional analysis per serving:
Calories 412, Protein 29 g, Carbohydrates 36 g, Fat 3 g,
Saturated Fat 1 g, Cholesterol 42 mg, Sodium 218 mg

You may use a combination of turkey and lean beef, but it will increase the level of fat.

Stuffed Cabbage

Prep
1 hr 24 min

Cook
50 min

Yields approximately 20 rolls

Ingredients

1 cup (240 ml) raw white rice
1 head cabbage
olive oil spray
½ lb (230 g) 90 percent extra-lean ground beef
½ lb (230 g) 99 percent lean ground turkey breast
½ cup (120 ml) Italian bread crumbs
¼ cup (60 ml) Parmesan cheese
¼ cup (60 ml) egg substitute
32-oz can (960 g) crushed tomatoes
5 cloves garlic, minced
1 teaspoon (5 ml) oregano
1 tablespoon (15 ml) parsley
1 teaspoon (5 ml) basil

Equipment

large pot
small pot
large frying pan
spoon
large bowl
knife
can opener
toothpicks

*This is one of my favorite dishes.
It's even better the second day!*

15 minutes	Bring large pot of water to a boil for the cabbage.
30 minutes	Bring 2 cups of water to a boil in a small pot, add rice, reduce heat to simmer and cover. Cook for 15–20 minutes until done.
6 minutes	Core cabbage. Immerse cabbage in water. Reduce heat. Cook for 5 minutes.
5 minutes	Remove cabbage from water. Handling cabbage carefully, peel leaves off and lay on paper towels to dry.
1 minute	Chop up small center leaves and set aside.
12 minutes	Spray frying pan with olive oil spray. Cook beef and turkey over medium heat breaking it up well with a fork. Drain excess grease.
5 minutes	Combine cooked ground meat, cooked rice, chopped cabbage, bread crumbs, parmesan cheese and egg substitute in bowl. Mix well.
20 minutes	Put a heaping tablespoon of the mixture in each leaf and roll up. Hold together with toothpick. Place in frying pan. Fill pan with the stuffed cabbage leaves.
5 minutes	Cover with crushed tomatoes, garlic and spices. Bring to a boil.
45 minutes	Reduce to simmer. Cover with lid or foil. Simmer 45 minutes.

Approximate nutritional analysis per 2-piece serving:
Calories 98, Protein 9 g, Carbohydrates 21 g, Fat 2 g,
Saturated Fat <1 g, Cholesterol 17 mg, Sodium 135 mg

Use this stuffing for peppers; bake them for an hour at 350 degrees.

Spanish Rice Dinner

Serves 6

Ingredients

olive oil spray
4 lean hot turkey sausages, cut into quarters
3 green chili peppers, seeded and minced
¾ lb (455 g) skinless chicken breast, cubed large
1 medium onion, chopped
6 cloves garlic, minced
2 cups (480 ml) low-sodium chicken stock, defatted
2 cups (480 ml) beer or non-alcoholic beer
1 small green pepper, seeded and diced
1 small red pepper, seeded and diced
2 medium tomatoes, seeded and diced
6 green Spanish olives, pitted and minced
2 cups (480 ml) long grain rice
1 teaspoon (5 ml) cilantro

½ teaspoon (3 ml) paprika
½ teaspoon (3 ml) tumeric
1 teaspoon (5 ml) salt
½ teaspoon (3 ml) pepper
1 large bay leaf
1 dozen medium shrimp, cleaned and peeled

Equipment

Dutch oven with lid (cast-iron pot)
knife
large spoon

This dish is even better the next day!

38

15 minutes	Prepare ingredients as listed.
10 minutes	Over medium heat, spray pot with olive oil spray. Brown sausage and chicken, set aside.
3 minutes	Spray pot with oil again, sauté onions until translucent; add garlic and chili peppers, cook one more minute.
25 minutes	Add stock and beer to pot. Bring to a boil. Add all other vegetables, rice and spices and return sausage and chicken. Cover and cook for 20 minutes.
5 minutes	Add shrimp to pot, stir and cover. Cook another five minutes or until shrimp is fully cooked, and orange but not curled tightly. Serve immediately.

Approximate nutritional analysis per serving:
Calories 297, Protein 24 g, Carbohydrates 11 g, Fat 6.5 g,
Saturated Fat 2 g, Cholesterol 88 mg, Sodium 544 mg

This dish doesn't freeze but keeps well in the refrigerator all week for quick meals.

Sprinkle with Tabasco and serve with hot tortillas.

Vegetable Lasagna

Serves 6

Ingredients

1 teaspoon (5 ml) vegetable oil

1 lb (455 g) lasagna noodles

olive oil spray

1 medium zucchini squash, julienned

2 large carrots, sliced thin

8-oz package (240 g) frozen leaf spinach; or fresh, steamed

2 cloves garlic, minced

salt and pepper

8 oz (240 g) nonfat ricotta

¼ cup (60 ml) egg substitute

¼ cup (60 ml) Parmesan, grated

¼ cup (60 ml) fresh parsley, chopped fine

½ cup (120 ml) skim milk mozzarella, grated

½ cup (120 ml) nonfat mozzarella, grated

12-oz can (360 ml) evaporated skim milk

1 tablespoon (15 ml) cornstarch

Equipment

large pot

small bowl

large frying pan

9 x 12-inch casserole dish

small saucepan

knife

grater

measuring cup and spoons

colander

Divide into single servings and freeze. Microwaves well.

40

15 minutes	Bring pot of water with teaspoon of oil to a boil.
	Prepare ingredients as listed.
5 minutes	Reduce heat under the water. Cook lasagna noodles until pliable, but not fully cooked.
5 minutes	Drain. Fill pot with cool water. Return noodles to water. Set aside.
10 minutes	Spray frying pan liberally with olive oil spray. Over medium heat, sauté zucchini and carrots for 5 minutes; add spinach and garlic, sauté 2 more minutes. Salt and pepper to taste. Set aside.
3 minutes	Mix together ricotta cheese, egg substitute, Parmesan cheese and parsley. Set aside.
1 minute	Combine skim milk and nonfat mozzarella cheeses. Set aside
5 minutes	In a small saucepan over medium heat, thicken the evaporated milk with cornstarch. Add salt and pepper.
1 minute	Drain pasta again.
	Spray the bottom of the casserole dish with olive oil spray.
10 minutes	Spoon some white sauce into the bottom of the pan. Make layers of noodles, then vegetables, then ricotta cheese mixture, then mozzarella, then spoon over some white sauce. Repeat three times or until casserole is full.
45 minutes	Bake for 45 minutes at 350 degrees (180°C).

Approximate nutritional analysis per serving:
Calories 388, Protein 28 g, Carbohydrates 69 g, Fat 4 g,
Saturated Fat 1 g, Cholesterol 22 mg, Sodium 289 mg

41

Chicken Sorrentino

Serves 4

Ingredients

1 lb (455 g) chicken breasts, pounded thin
½ cup (120 ml) grated skim milk mozzarella
½ cup (120 ml) grated nonfat mozzarella
2 tablespoons (30 ml) Parmesan cheese, grated
¼ cup (60 ml) flour
olive oil spray
¼ lb (115 g) 97 percent fat-free ham, chopped
3 cloves garlic, peeled and chopped
¼ cup (60 ml) dry red wine, optional
¼ teaspoon (1 ml) dried oregano
¼ teaspoon (1 ml) dried basil
1 teaspoon (5 ml) dried or fresh parsley
1 cup (240 ml) fat-free tomato pasta sauce
salt and pepper to taste

Equipment

large frying pan
grater
can opener
measuring cup and spoons
mallet
wax paper
knife
sifter
spatula

*This recipe is also great with veal,
but will contain more saturated fat.*

42

20 minutes	Pound the chicken thin between sheets of wax paper.
1 minute	Combine all cheese in a bowl and set aside.
2 minutes	Flour the chicken on both sides shaking off excess. Set aside.
5 minutes	Spray frying pan with olive oil spray. Over medium heat, lay breasts in pan. Cook one side for 3 minutes. Turn over, cook for 2 minutes. Put ham and garlic into middle of pan and sauté 1 minute as chicken cooks. Put mixture on top of chicken. Add wine, sprinkle with spices.
12 minutes	Top chicken with cheese, spoon over pasta sauce. Cover with lid or foil and lower heat. Simmer for 10 minutes while cheese melts, sauce gets heated and chicken cooks through. Season to taste.

Serve alone or with pasta.

Approximate nutritional analysis per serving:
Calories 288, Protein 51 g, Carbohydrates 8 g, Fat 5.5 g,
Saturated Fat 2.5 g, Cholesterol 98 mg, Sodium 466 mg

Have some pounded chicken breasts and homemade sauce in the freezer to make this recipe in a flash!

Crab Cakes

Serves 4

Ingredients

1 lb (455 g) lump crab meat, picked clean of shell
1 tablespoon (15 ml) low-fat mayonnaise
1 tablespoon (15 ml) Dijon mustard
1 teaspoon (5 ml) Worcestershire sauce
¼ cup (60 ml) scallions, finely diced
¼ cup (60 ml) red pepper, finely diced
¼ cup (60 ml) egg substitute or 2 egg whites
¼ cup (60 ml) fresh bread crumbs
3 tablespoons (45 ml) unbleached white flour
olive oil spray

Equipment

large mixing bowl
large nonstick frying pan
spatula
large spoon

These make a great appetizer as well as main course. Or make them smaller for fancy hors d'oeuvres.

44

10 minutes	Prepare ingredients as listed.
1 minute	In a large mixing bowl flake the crab meat but not too finely (some people enjoy getting sizeable chunks in their cakes).
2 minutes	In a separate bowl mix together the mayonnaise, mustard and Worcestershire and add it to the crab meat. Add the scallions, red pepper, egg substitute and bread crumbs.
20-30 minutes	Refrigerate the mixture for 20 to 30 minutes to firm up.
5 minutes	Scoop a heaping tablespoon of the crab and mold it into a pancake about 1 inch thick. Dust with the flour and set aside.
12 minutes	Heat pan over a medium heat, spray with olive oil spray. Fry one side of the crab cakes until golden brown, turn over and coat cake with cooking spray and cook until golden and heated through.

Serve with fat-free spicy salsa.

Approximate nutritional analysis per serving:
Calories 207, Protein 29 g, Carbohydrates 12 g, Fat 2 g,
Saturated Fat <1 g, Cholesterol 79 mg, Sodium 215 mg

If you don't like red peppers you can substitute another crunchy vegetable, green peppers or even carrots.

Spinach Fettucini Alfredo

Serves 4-6

Ingredients

1 lb (455 g) spinach fettucini
2 cloves garlic, flattened
olive oil spray
1 tablespoon (15 ml) low-fat margarine
2 tablespoons (30 ml) sifted flour
12-oz can (360 ml) evaporated skim milk
½ cup (120 ml) buttermilk
2 teaspoons (10 ml) butter substitute flakes
3 tablespoons (45 ml) fresh Parmesan, grated
salt and pepper to taste
1 tablespoon (15 ml) dried parsley

Equipment

large pot
small saucepan
colander
large bowl
sifter
can opener
wide knife
measuring cup and spoons
pasta utensils

Sauté or steam vegetables like broccoli and mushrooms and add them to the sauce for a one-dish meal.

46

10 minutes	Prepare ingredients as listed.
15 minutes	Bring salted water to a boil in large pot.
12 minutes	Reduce heat and cook fettucini until it is al dente.
1 minute	Drain in colander. Fill the pot with cool water and return the hot pasta to the water. Set aside.
	Flatten the garlic by slamming with the blade of a wide knife on a cutting board.
2 minutes	Spray the small saucepan liberally with olive oil spray. Over medium heat, sauté the garlic for a minute or two moving them around constantly. Do not burn!
2 minutes	Add the margarine and melt it. Remove the garlic from the sauce pan. Add the flour and stir to make a paste. Lower the heat.
5 minutes	Slowly add the evaporated milk and then the buttermilk, whisking constantly as it thickens.
2 minutes	Add the butter flakes and Parmesan cheese. Continue to whisk as it thickens more. Salt and pepper to taste.
2 minutes	Drain the pasta again. Put into a large serving bowl and pour the Alfredo sauce over it. Toss, garnish with parsley, serve.

Approximate nutritional analysis per serving:
Calories 557, Protein 24 g, Carbohydrates 97 g, Fat 4.5 g,
Saturated Fat 2 g, Cholesterol 8 mg, Sodium 313 mg

Alfredo sauce tastes great on many kinds of pasta.

Fillet of Sole Meunière

Serves 4

Ingredients

1 lb (455 g) sole fillets
olive oil spray
¼ cup (60 ml) sifted flour
2 cloves garlic, minced
juice of one lemon, reserve rind
¼ cup (60 ml) white wine
1 teaspoon (5 ml) dried oregano
1 teaspoon (5 ml) dried parsley
1 teaspoon (5 ml) butter substitute flakes diluted in
    1 tablespoon (15 ml) warm water, or low-fat margarine
1 teaspoon (5 ml) Dijon mustard
salt and pepper
¼ teaspoon (1 ml) lemon rind
fresh parsley for garnish

Equipment

medium frying pan
2 small bowls
grater
measuring cup and spoons
sifter
knife

I like to serve fish with rice. Try the Vegetable Rice recipe!

48

15 minutes	Prepare ingredients as listed.
	Rinse fish and pat dry.
	Heat frying pan over medium flame. Spray liberally with olive oil spray.
5 minutes	Flour fish fillets on both sides, shaking off any excess. Place in frying pan.
8-10 minutes	Cook for 4-5 minutes on each side or until done. (Don't let fillets brown.) Remove and set aside.
5 minutes	In the same pan (do not clean it) sauté the garlic for 1 minute. Add the lemon juice, wine, spices, butter substitute flakes and mustard. Raise the heat and bring to a boil whisking quickly to incorporate all ingredients (including any floury remains from cooking the fish). Let thicken slightly, (1-2 minutes, careful don't let it all evaporate). Salt and pepper to taste.
2 minutes	Lower the heat to a low simmer. Return the fish to the pan, spoon over the sauce. Warm the fish 1-2 minutes.
	Serve garnished with lemon rind and fresh parsley.

Approximate nutritional analysis per serving:
Calories 158, Protein 22 g, Carbohydrates 7 g, Fat 4 g,
Saturated Fat <1 g, Cholesterol 54 mg, Sodium 122 mg

Any mild white fish will do here!

Linguini Carbonara

Serves 4-6

Ingredients

1 lb (455 g) linguini
olive oil spray
1 small onion finely diced
6 oz (180 g) 97 percent fat-free ham, chopped
1 cup (240 ml) egg substitute
2 tablespoons (30 ml) Parmesan cheese, grated
salt and pepper

Equipment

large pot
colander
whisk
knife
utensils to toss
measuring cup and spoons

Add some of your favorite vegetables, lightly steamed, for a complete meal.

50

10 minutes	Bring water to a boil in a large pot. Prepare ingredients as listed.
12-15 minutes	Reduce heat. Cook linguini until it is al dente, approximately 12 minutes. Drain, spray with olive oil spray and toss so it doesn't stick. Return to the pot, cover and keep warm.
5 minutes	In the same pot over medium heat, spray with olive oil spray. Sauté onion until translucent. Add ham and sauté 1 more minute.
3 minutes	Pour in egg substitute. Whisk as it starts to cook. When the egg is half cooked, return linguini to the pot. Add Parmesan, salt and pepper to taste.
3-5 minutes	Toss until egg is totally cooked and pasta is hot.

Serve immediately.

Approximate nutritional analysis per serving:
Calories 564, Protein 33 g, Carbohydrates 84 g, Fat 6 g,
Saturated Fat 1 g, Cholesterol 22 mg, Sodium 780 mg

Try turkey bacon or turkey salami instead of ham.

Sesame Noodles

Serves 6

Ingredients

6 oz (180 g) fresh bean sprouts, blanched
1 lb (460 g) whole wheat or buckwheat noodles
2 tablespoons (30 ml) reduced-fat peanut butter
3 tablespoons (45 ml) low-sodium soy sauce
1½ tablespoons (23 ml) red wine vinegar
1 tablespoon (15 ml) sesame oil
1 teaspoon (5 ml) chili oil, optional
1 teaspoon (5 ml) cayenne pepper
6 scallions, finely sliced

Equipment

large pot (for boiling pasta)
small pot
small bowl
large bowl
whisk
knife
colander

Great as an appetizer or light lunch.

52

5 minutes	Blanch sprouts by dipping them in boiling water for 1 minute, then drain and cool.
10-12 minutes	Bring water to a boil in a large pot and cook noodles.
2 minutes	In a bowl, add peanut butter, soy sauce, vinegar, sesame oil, chili oil, if desired and cayenne pepper. Blend well with whisk.
3 minutes	Drain noodles and put in large bowl. Add peanut sauce while noodles are hot and toss vigorously, mixing it well.
5 minutes	Let cool slightly. Add sprouts and scallions. Toss again.

Serve warm or cold.

Approximate nutritional analysis per serving:
Calories 187, Protein 12 g, Carbohydrates 23 g, Fat 7 g,
Saturated Fat 1 g, Cholesterol 0 mg, Sodium 520 mg

My sister Julie loves to eat this cold.

Shrimp Scampi

Serves 4

Ingredients

butter-flavored oil spray
1 tablespoon (15 ml) extra virgin olive oil
4 cloves garlic, minced
1 lb (455 g) large shrimp, cleaned and deveined
pinch red pepper flakes
1 teaspoon (5 ml) dried oregano
1 teaspoon (5 ml) dried basil
¼ cup (60 ml) dry white wine
⅓ cup (80 ml) clam juice
juice ¼ lemon
½ lb (255 g) capellini cooked until al dente and kept warm

Equipment

large frying pan
knife
juicer dish
measuring cup and spoons

This is one of my favorite recipes, tasty and fast.

54

15 minutes	Prepare ingredients as listed.
1 minute	Over medium heat, spray the pan with butter-flavored spray. Add olive oil. Sauté garlic lightly.
2 minutes	Add shrimp and spices. Cook shrimp 2 minutes until tails begin to curl.
5 minutes	Turn shrimp over. Add wine, clam juice and lemon juice. Raise heat to high. Bring sauce to a boil while shrimp continues to cook.
	Remove shrimp to a warm plate.
2 minutes	Reduce sauce on high heat 1-2 minutes. Pour over shrimp.
	Serve over capellini or liguini.

Approximate nutritional analysis per serving with ½ lb pasta:
Calories 374, Protein 37 g, Carbohydrates 69 g, Fat 4 g,
Saturated Fat <1 g, Cholesterol 172 mg, Sodium 169 mg

Steam open any shellfish in a little water, and add it to the sauce for shellfish scampi.

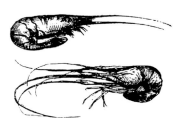

Delicious over rice too!

Caesar Salad

Serves 6

Ingredients

5 cloves fresh garlic, minced
1 tin flat anchovies, rinsed and minced
¼ cup (60 ml) egg substitute
1 teaspoon (5 ml) Dijon mustard
1 tablespoon (15 ml) Worcestershire sauce
juice of one lemon
3 tablespoons (45 ml) extra virgin olive oil
¼ cup white (60 ml) wine vinegar
¼ cup (60 ml) plain nonfat yogurt
1 large head of romaine lettuce washed
    and cut into 1-inch strips
1 cup (240 ml) nonfat croutons
¼ cup (60 ml) Parmesan cheese, grated
salt and pepper

Equipment

lettuce washer
knife
wooden salad bowl
measuring cup and spoons
citrus juicer dish or fork and strainer

Slice a baked chicken breast over the top and you have a whole meal in one.

56

15 minutes	Prepare all ingredients as listed.
5 minutes	In the bottom of the wooden bowl put garlic, anchovies, egg substitute, mustard, Worcestershire sauce, lemon juice, olive oil, vinegar and yogurt. Mix well.
5 minutes	Add lettuce and croutons and toss. Sprinkle Parmesan cheese over top and toss until lettuce is well coated. Season to taste.

Approximate nutritional analysis per serving:
Calories 145, Protein 9 g, Carbohydrates 7 g, Fat 8 g,
Saturated Fat 2 g, Cholesterol 12 mg, Sodium 521 mg

We eat this salad on a regular basis as a meal or just as a starter.

Add ripe cherry tomatoes to the salad.

Carrot Salad

Serves 8

Ingredients

½ cup (120 ml) gold raisins, soaked
¼ cup (60 ml) of orange juice
3 cups (720 ml) carrots, washed and julienned
1 cup (240 ml) celery, finely sliced
¼ cup (60 ml) lemon juice
1 teaspoon (5 ml) fresh Italian parsley, finely chopped
½ teaspoon (3 ml) salt
½ teaspoon (3 ml) white pepper
1 tablespoon (15 ml) extra virgin olive oil

Equipment

food processor or hand shredder
large mixing bowl
small mixing bowl
knife
measuring cups and spoons
slotted spoon or colander
utensils for tossing

This recipe was created with the help of my mother-in-law!

58

Soak raisins in orange juice for 30 minutes in the small mixing bowl.

15 minutes Scrub the carrots well to remove all dirt; julienne, then set aside.

15 minutes Slice celery thinly. Chop the parsley.

5 minutes Drain raisins (discard orange juice) and combine all ingredients in the large mixing bowl. Toss well.

1 hour Mix well, refrigerate for at least an hour.

Approximate nutritional analysis per serving:
Calories 68, Protein <1 g, Carbohydrates 13 g, Fat 2 g,
Saturated Fat <1 g, Cholesterol 0 mg, Sodium 162 mg

Try other fruits such as dried apricots or fresh diced pineapple instead of raisins for a tropical taste.

Legume Salad

Serves 10

Ingredients

1½ cups (355 ml) cooked red kidney beans, fresh or canned
1½ cups (355 ml) cooked white navy beans,
    fresh or canned
1½ cups (355 ml) cooked chickpeas, fresh or canned
1½ cups (355 ml) cooked black beans, fresh or canned
4 cloves fresh garlic, minced
1 small white onion, diced finely
1 small red pepper, cleaned and diced finely
½ small green pepper, cleaned and diced finely
2 tablespoons (30 ml) fresh parsley, chopped
3 tablespoons (45 ml) extra virgin olive oil
2 tablespoons (30 ml) fresh lemon juice
¼ cup (60 ml) plain nonfat yogurt
salt and pepper to taste

Equipment

large mixing bowl
knife
measuring cup and spoons

This salad gets better and better the longer it is refrigerated.

60

15 minutes Prepare ingredients as listed.

Combine all ingredients into a bowl. Mix well and refrigerate overnight so the flavors can marry—couldn't be easier!

When cooking beans yourself, keep in mind that approximately ¾ cup dry beans will equal 1½ cups cooked beans. I find using canned beans much easier in this recipe, since otherwise each of the beans included has different cooking times and needs to be cooked separately.

Approximate nutritional analysis per serving:
Calories 209, Protein 11 g, Carbohydrates 31 g, Fat 4.5 g,
Saturated Fat <1 g, Cholesterol <1 mg, Sodium 7 mg

Try using your favorite lowfat vinaigrette instead of the dressing called for here for a different flavor.

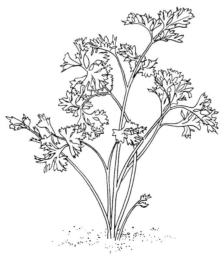

Macaroni Salad

Serves 8 as a side dish

Ingredients

1 lb (455 g) of elbow macaroni
4 large scallions, finely sliced
1 tablespoon (15 ml) fresh dill, finely minced
½ small red pepper, seeded and finely diced
1 heaping tablespoon (15 ml) sweet relish
1 cup (240 ml) nonfat mayonnaise spread
1 teaspoon (5 ml) Dijon mustard
salt and pepper

Equipment

4-quart pot
colander
large mixing bowl
sharp knife
measuring cups and spoons

*Add chicken or beef to the salad
for a complete light summer meal.*

15 minutes	Fill pot with water and bring to a boil. Prepare vegetables and ingredients as stated above.
15 minutes	Add macaroni and lower to a high simmer. Cook pasta until done, about 12 to 15 minutes.
5 minutes	Drain pasta and rinse with cold water until cooled. Drain again.
5 minutes	In the mixing bowl combine pasta, scallions, dill, red pepper, sweet relish, mayonnaise and mustard. Mix well. Salt and pepper to taste.

Serve immediately or chill.

Approximate nutritional analysis per serving:
Calories 203, Protein 6 g, Carbohydrates 35 g, Fat 0 g,
Saturated Fat 0 g, Cholesterol 12 mg, Sodium 36 mg

Try using different kinds of pasta, rotini or colored varieties, for a more exciting presentation.

Salad Tricolore

Serves 6

Ingredients

10 cups of radicchio lettuce, chopped into medium pieces,
    endive leaves, cut into ½-inch slices and
    romaine lettuce, cut into ½-inch slices

6 plum tomatoes, seeded and diced

1 cucumber, seeded and cubed

6 leaves fresh basil, minced

4 oz (120 g) nonfat mozzarella, finely cubed
    or 2 oz skim milk mozzarella

juice of ½ lemon

salt and pepper to taste

Equipment

wooden bowl

knife

salad tongs

Fabulous on a hot summer day or with a bowl of hot soup in the winter.

64

15 minutes	Prepare all vegetables and basil.
1 minute	Dice mozzarella and put everything into a salad bowl.
1 minute	Squeeze on lemon juice and add salt and pepper.
10 minutes	Refrigerate for 10 minutes.

Approximate nutritional analysis per serving:
Calories 58, Protein 8 g, Carbohydrates 7 g, Fat <1 g,
Saturated Fat 0 g, Cholesterol 3 mg, Sodium 13 mg

Add white cannelli beans in this salad for a hearty meal.

Add your favorite low-calorie dressing or choose one from this book!

Balsamic Dressing

Serves 6

Ingredients
¼ cup (60 ml) balsamic vinegar
½ cup (120 ml) plain nonfat yogurt
3 whole scallions, diced
3 cloves of fresh garlic, minced
1 tablespoon (15 ml) fresh or dried rosemary
¼ teaspoon (1 ml) salt
¼ teaspoon (1 ml) pepper
⅛ cup (40 ml) spring water

Equipment
blender or hand mixer
measuring cups and spoons
bowl

This pretty dressing works well as a dip for crudités. Omit the water for a thicker consistency.

10 minutes   Prepare all ingredients as listed.

1 minute   Blend all ingredients until smooth, though scallion greens should appear as flecks. The finished dressing should have bits of scallion and garlic in it.

Refrigerate until ready to use.

Approximate nutritional analysis per serving:
Calories 13, Protein 1 g, Carbohydrates 2 g, Fat <1 g,
Saturated Fat <1 g, Cholesterol <1 mg, Sodium 101 mg

Throw in a tablespoon of no-salt dried vegetable seasoning for a more diverse flavor.

Blue Cheese Dressing

Serves 12

Ingredients

1 cup (240 ml) low-fat buttermilk
2 oz (60 g) nonfat cream cheese
½ cup (120 ml) fat-free sour cream
½ cup (120 ml) low-fat mayonnaise dressing
2 tablespoons (30 ml) white wine vinegar
½ teaspoon (3 ml) garlic powder
½ teaspoon (3 ml) onion powder
1 teaspoon (5 ml) salt
1 teaspoon (5 ml) black pepper
1 tablespoon (15 ml) fresh parsley, finely chopped
¼ teaspoon (1 ml) dried marjoram
½ teaspoon (3 ml) Dijon mustard
3 oz (90 g) blue cheese, finely crumbled

Equipment

blender or hand mixer
measuring cups and spoons
knife
bowl

Try this dressing with Buffalo chicken wings but remember to remove the chicken skin!

68

5 minutes	Prepare ingredients as listed.
2 minutes	Blend all ingredients together except for blue cheese.
1 minute	Stir in crumbled blue cheese.
	Refrigerate overnight, if possible..

Approximate nutritional analysis per serving:
Calories 56, Protein 4 g, Carbohydrates 2 g, Fat 3 g,
Saturated Fat 1.2 g, Cholesterol 12 mg, Sodium 346 mg

I, love this with cold celery as a tasty satisfying snack.

This dressing is great for dips.

Lemon–Ginger Vinaigrette

Serves 6

Ingredients

¼ cup (60 ml) lemon juice
1 teaspoon (5 ml) lemon rind, grated
1 teaspoon (5 ml) fresh ginger, peeled and diced finely
1 tablespoon (15 ml) Dijon mustard
3 tablespoon (45 ml) cold spring water
pepper to taste

Equipment

grater
juicer dish (or fork and strainer)
whisk
bowl
measuring spoons and cup

So quick and delicious, who needs bottled dressing?

10 minutes Prepare ingredients as listed above.

Whisk all ingredients together well.

Toss into salad and serve.

Approximate nutritional analysis per serving:
Calories 7, Protein <1 g, Carbohydrates 2 g, Fat 0 g,
Saturated Fat 0 g, Cholesterol 0 mg, Sodium 49 mg

This dressing would be great over a green bean salad!

Buttermilk Dressing

Serves 8

Ingredients

1 cup (240 ml) low-fat buttermilk
½ cup (120 ml) nonfat or
    50 percent reduced-fat sour cream
1 teaspoon (5 ml) Dijon mustard
1 tablespoon (15 ml) fresh dill, minced
2 cloves fresh garlic, minced
1 teaspoon (5 ml) black pepper
2 tablespoons (30 ml) minced onion

Equipment

knife
whisk
bowl
measuring cups and spoons

10 minutes   Prepare ingredients as listed.

1 minute   Whisk together all ingredients. Refrigerate until ready to serve.

Approximate nutritional analysis per serving:
Calories 30, Protein 3 g, Carbohydrates 3 g, Fat <1 g,
Saturated Fat <1 g, Cholesterol 1 mg, Sodium 64 mg

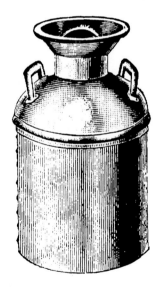

Parmesan Dressing

Serves 8

Ingredients

½ cup (120 ml) Parmesan, finely grated
½ cup (120 ml) low-fat mayonnaise dressing
½ cup (120 ml) nonfat sour cream
½ cup (120 ml) low-fat milk
1 teaspoon (5 ml) Dijon mustard
½ teaspoon (3 ml) garlic powder
½ teaspoon (3 ml) onion powder
1 teaspoon (5 ml) dried parsley
1 teaspoon (5 ml) black pepper
salt to taste

Equipment

blender or hand mixer
measuring cups and spoons
bowl

Add more milk for thinner dressing, less for a thicker dressing.

74

5 minutes   Prepare ingredients as listed.

2 minutes   Whisk all ingredients together until smooth.

Refrigerate until ready to serve.

Approximate nutritional analysis per serving:
Calories 63, Protein 5 g, Carbohydrates 2 g, Fat 4 g,
Saturated Fat 2 g, Cholesterol 13 mg, Sodium 157 mg

I like this spread thinly on a slice of Italian or French bread broiled until slightly brown and bubbly. Yummy!

Another great dip!

Thousand Island Dressing

Serves 6

Ingredients

1 cup (240 ml) low-fat or nonfat mayonnaise dressing
¼ cup (60 ml) ketchup
2 tablespoons (30 ml) sweet relish

Equipment

measuring cup and spoons
bowl
spoon

This is the dressing most likely to get your children to eat their salads!

1 minute   Whisk all ingredients together.

Serve.

Approximate nutritional analysis per 1 tbs serving:
Calories 36, Protein <1 g, Carbohydrates 3 g, Fat 1 g,
Saturated Fat <1 g, Cholesterol 10 mg, Sodium 102 mg

This is also great as a sandwich spread!

Couldn't be simpler!

Best Beans

Serves 10

Ingredients

1½ cups (355 ml) dry red kidney beans
1½ cups (355 ml) dry white canelli beans
14 oz (420 ml) reduced sodium low-fat beef broth, defatted
3 cups (720 ml) water
4 drops artificial smoke flavoring, optional
2 slices turkey bacon, diced, or 1 tablespoon
    artificial bacon bits
¼ cup (60 ml) tomato paste
3 whole bay leaves
4 cloves garlic, sliced
1 teaspoon (5 ml) cumin
1 teaspoon (5 ml) Tabasco
salt and pepper to taste

Equipment

large mixing bowl
3-quart saucepan
measuring cup and spoons

This dish takes a while to cook, filling the house with a wonderful aroma, but is little work—my kind of cooking!

1 hour Rinse the dry beans in a bowl full of water, pick out any stones or foreign matter that floats to the top. Either soak overnight, covered with water, or cover beans with boiling water for 1 hour.

2½–3 hours Put all ingredients in a saucepan. Bring to a boil and stir until tomato paste has dissolved. Reduce heat and simmer for 2½–3 hours. Stir often and don't let liquid evaporate. If it does, add water and reduce heat.

Approximate nutritional analysis per serving:
Calories 209, Protein 15 g, Carbohydrates 37 g, Fat 1 g,
Saturated Fat 0 g, Cholesterol 3 mg, Sodium 74 mg

Use canned beans for faster preparation, but use less salt and reduce the cooking time to 45 minutes.

Vegetable Rolls with Mustard Sauce ❧❧❧❧❧

Makes approximately 40 pieces

Ingredients
olive oil spray
5 scallions, finely sliced
¼ cup (60 ml) low-sodium chicken broth, defatted
3 cloves garlic, minced
½ cup (120 ml) mushrooms, chopped
2 large carrots, shredded
¼ cup (60 ml) red pepper, seeded and minced
1 tablespoon (15 ml) fresh ginger, peeled and minced
1 cup (240 ml) cooked spinach, fresh or frozen, chopped
2 cups (480 ml) bean sprouts, chopped
4 oz (120 g) firm tofu, finely chopped
1 teaspoon (5 ml) reduced-sodium soy sauce
1 package wonton wrappers

Dipping Sauce
¼ cup (60 ml) yellow mustard
2 tablespoons (30 ml) reduced-sodium soy sauce
¼ teaspoon (1 ml) hot chili oil, optional

Equipment
large nonstick skillet
vegetable grater
knife
measuring cup and spoons
cookie sheet
can opener

These rolls make fabulous hors d'oevures!

80

Preheat oven to 350 degrees (180°C).

20 minutes   Prepare all ingredients as listed above.

3 minutes   Spray skillet with olive oil spray. Over medium heat, sauté scallions for 2 minutes. Add a tablespoon of the chicken broth, then the garlic and sauté for another minute.

7 minutes   Add the carrots, red pepper, mushrooms, ginger, spinach and sprouts. Sauté for a few minutes until softened. Add tofu and pour in the remaining chicken broth. Raise heat and bring to a boil, cooking down until most of the liquid has evaporated. Season with a teaspoon of soy sauce.

10 minutes   Let vegetables cool.

15 minutes   Lay wonton wrapper on flat dry surface. Place a teaspoon of the vegetable mixture at one end and roll up into a tube shape. Pinch each end together and set aside on oil-sprayed cookie sheet close together but not touching.

30 minutes   When the tray is full, spray the top of each roll with olive oil spray and bake until golden, about 30 minutes.

Serve hot with chilled Dipping Sauce (combine ingredients and stir well).

Approximate nutritional analysis per serving
of 1 roll with 1 tsp dipping sauce:
Calories 33, Protein 1 g, Carbohydrates 6 g, Fat <1 g,
Saturated Fat <1 g, Cholesterol <1 mg, Sodium 194 mg

You can find wonton wrappers in the refrigerated section of your grocery.

Phyllo Mushroom Pies

Makes 16 pies

Ingredients

½ package phyllo dough leaves
1 tablespoon (15 ml) low-fat margarine
2 tablespoons (30 ml) unbleached white flour
olive oil spray
1 small onion, minced
2 cloves garlic, minced
4 oz (120 g) regular mushrooms, sliced
4 oz (120 g) crimini mushrooms, sliced
4 oz (120 g) portobello mushrooms, sliced
4 oz (120 g) oyster mushrooms, sliced (or use only two or
    three varieties to make up 1 lb (455 g))
¼ cup (60 ml) beef or chicken broth, canned or fresh
salt and pepper to taste
butter-flavor oil spray

Equipment

large frying pan
knife
can opener
2 cookie sheets

Smaller versions of these pies make great hors d'oeuvres for parties.

82

15 minutes	Prepare all ingredients as listed. Unfold phyllo dough carefully and lay out flat.
2 minutes	Soften the margarine and use your fingertips to blend in the flour to make a roux.
5 minutes	Spray the frying pan liberally with olive oil spray. Over medium heat, sauté onion until translucent. Add garlic, sauté 1 more minute.
10 minutes	Add the mushrooms and beef broth. Sauté until mushrooms juices are released and mushrooms are cooked. Add small amount of the roux, whisking continuously until the broth is very thick. Season to taste.
	Preheat oven to 350 degrees (180°C).
15 minutes	Let the mushrooms cool.
20 minutes	Lay out one leaf of phyllo. Cut in half, lengthwise. Spray the leaf with butter-flavored oil spray. Spoon out ¼ cup of the mushrooms onto the corner of the bottom of the dough. Fold over the corner. Fold side to side making a triangle until you get to the end of the dough. Repeat for the remainder of phyllo and mushroom mixture.
20-30 minutes	Spray cookie sheet with oil spray and arrange pies on sheet. Bake at 350 degrees (180°C) until golden brown. 20 to 30 minutes.

Approximate nutritional analysis per 1 pie serving:
Calories 104, Protein 3 g, Carbohydrates 18 g, Fat <1 g,
Saturated Fat <1 g, Cholesterol 0 mg, Sodium 147 mg

You can freeze the extra phyllo dough, and also freeze the pies for tasty treats in minutes.

Polenta and Vegetable Casserole

Serves 8

Ingredients

5 cups (1.2 l) spring water
2 teaspoons (10 ml) salt
olive oil spray
1 medium onion, thinly sliced
4 cloves garlic, sliced
1 medium green pepper, seeded and diced
1 medium red pepper, seeded and diced
2 cups (480 ml) mushrooms, sliced
1 medium zucchini, thickly sliced
1 medium yellow squash, thickly sliced
¼ teaspoon (1 ml) oregano
¼ teaspoon (1 ml) basil
¼ teaspoon (1 ml) paprika

1⅔ cups (400 ml) yellow cornmeal
3 tablespoons (45 ml) Parmesan cheese, grated
salt and pepper to taste

Equipment

large nonstick frying pan
9 x 12-inch casserole
large saucepan
whisk
knife
measuring cup and spoons

Melt reduced-fat cheddar over the top for a cheesier flavor.

Preheat oven to 325 degrees (165°C).

20 minutes   Prepare ingredients as listed.

Bring the water and salt to a boil in the saucepan.

10 minutes   Over medium heat, spray pan with olive oil spray. Sauté onion until translucent; stir in garlic for 1 minute. Add remaining vegetables, oregano, basil, paprika, salt and pepper to taste. Cook until vegetables are tender.

1 minute   Spoon vegetables into olive oil-sprayed casserole dish and set aside.

10 minutes   When the water is boiling, slowly add the cornmeal a little at a time, whisking constantly until all has been blended in. Whisk in the Parmesan cheese.

1 minute   Pour cornmeal mixture over vegetables and spread smooth.

15 minutes   Bake for 15 minutes or until polenta is lightly browned.

Serve immediately.

Approximate nutritional analysis per serving:
Calories 143, Protein 5 g, Carbohydrates 28 g, Fat 1 g,
Saturated Fat <1 g, Cholesterol 2 mg, Sodium 581 mg

The texture of this dish is enhanced by cutting the vegetables into various shapes and sizes.

CORN MEAL

Seasoned String Beans

Serves 6

Ingredients

olive oil spray

2 small chili peppers, seeded and minced

1 lb (455 g) string beans, cut in thirds

2 cloves garlic, minced

¼ cup (60 ml) white wine

1 tablespoon (15 ml) tomato paste

¼ teaspoon (1 ml) ground ginger

salt and pepper to taste

Equipment

large nonstick frying pan

knife

measuring spoons

spatula

These are an excellent accompaniment to grilled chicken or fish.

15 minutes	Prepare ingredients as listed.
3 minutes	Spray frying pan with olive oil spray. Over medium heat, sauté chili peppers for 1 minute, add green beans and garlic and cook for 2 more minutes.
10-12 minutes	Add wine, tomato paste and ginger. Season to taste. Sauté until the liquid evaporates by half but still coats the string beans. Don't let the string beans overcook. They should remain slightly firm.

Serve.

Approximate nutritional analysis per serving:
Calories 36, Protein 2 g, Carbohydrates 6 g, Fat <1 g,
Saturated Fat <1 g, Cholesterol 0 mg, Sodium 7 mg

Spicy Chick-Peas

Serves 8

Ingredients

2 cups (480 ml) dried chick-peas or
    3 cups (720 ml) canned chick-peas
olive oil spray
1 medium onion, finely chopped
3 cloves garlic, minced
2 small chili peppers, seeded and minced
1 tablespoon (15 ml) fresh ginger, peeled and minced
1 cup (240 ml) plum tomatoes, seeded and diced
½ lemon, juiced
1 cup (240 ml) spring water

Equipment

medium saucepan
medium bowl
knife
measuring cup and spoons
juicer
(can opener)

This dish is great served cold with pita bread.

88

1 hour	In medium saucepan, cover chick-peas with water and bring to a boil. Cook at high simmer for 1 hour until tender but not mushy. Drain. If using canned chick-peas, rinse and drain them.
10 minutes	Prepare ingredients as listed.
5 minutes	Spray pan with olive oil spray. Over medium heat, sauté onions, garlic and chili peppers for 5 minutes. Be careful not to burn garlic.
35 minutes	Add ginger, tomatoes, lemon juice and water; bring to a boil. Add chick-peas. Simmer for 30 minutes.

Approximate nutritional analysis per serving:
Calories 161, Protein 8 g, Carbohydrates 28 g, Fat 1.5 g,
Saturated Fat <1 g, Cholesterol 0 mg, Sodium 56 mg

A great complement to any chicken, meat or fish dish, or serve as a main course with rice.

Vegetable Fried Rice

Serves 8

Prep 25 min

Cook 20 min

Ingredients

1 medium onion, diced
½ small green pepper, seeded and diced
3 cloves garlic, minced
1 tablespoon (15 ml) extra virgin olive oil
2 cups (480 ml) long grain white rice
olive oil spray, if necessary
1 medium carrot, grated and chopped
4 cups (960 ml) spring water
salt and pepper to taste

Equipment

medium saucepan
knife
measuring cup and spoons

Add chicken broth in place of water for a more intense flavor.

15 minutes	Prepare ingredients as listed.
5 minutes	Over medium heat, sauté the onions, peppers and garlic in the olive oil until the onions are translucent.
5 minutes	Add the rice and sauté until the rice is coated with the oil and begins to darken slightly in color. Spray the rice with more oil spray if necessary.
	Add the water, carrots and seasoning. Cover and bring to a boil, then reduce to a simmer.
20 minutes	Simmer for 20 minutes or until all the water is absorbed and the rice is tender.

Approximate nutritional analysis per serving:
Calories 188, Protein 4 g, Carbohydrates 40 g, Fat <1 g,
Saturated Fat <1 g, Cholesterol 0 mg, Sodium 6 mg

Cook the rice with slices of chicken or lean beef for a complete meal in a pot.

Vegetable Pancakes

Yields 3 dozen pancakes

Prep
15 min

Cook
20 min

Ingredients

2 cups (480 ml) potatoes with skins, shredded
½ cup (120 ml) onion, shredded
1 cup (240 ml) carrot, shredded
1 cup (240 ml) yellow squash, shredded
1 cup (240 ml) zucchini, shredded
½ cup (120 ml) egg substitute (or 3 egg whites)
3 tablespoons (45 ml) unbleached white flour
¾ teaspoon (5 ml) baking powder
1 teaspoon (5 ml) pepper
½ teaspoon (3 ml) salt
olive oil spray

Equipment

food processor with shredder
nonstick skillet
large mixing bowl
colander
measuring cup and spoons
spatula

Great as hors d'oeuvres made as bite-sized pancakes.

15 minutes	Shred potatoes first and set aside in colander in sink to drain. Prepare all remaining ingredients as listed.
5 minutes	In the mixing bowl, combine all vegetables with the egg substitute, flour, baking soda, salt and pepper. Mix well.
25 minutes	Over medium heat, spray skillet with olive oil spray. When pan is hot, spoon a heaping tablespoon of vegetables into pan and flatten. Cook on both sides until brown and firm. (Continue to spray the pan with oil so they don't stick.) Keep warm on foil in the oven until all are cooked. Serve hot.

Approximate nutritional analysis per 1 pancake serving:
Calories 43, Protein 2 g, Carbohydrates 8 g, Fat <1 g,
Saturated Fat <1 g, Cholesterol 0 mg, Sodium 87 mg

These pancakes freeze well for a few months.

Serve with applesauce
and/or reduced-fat sour cream.

Wild, Wild Rice

Serves 6

Ingredients

olive oil spray
2 cloves garlic, minced
1 small onion, chopped
1 small chili pepper, seeded and minced, optional
1 cup (240 ml) brown rice
1 teaspoon (5 ml) spicy seasoning salt substitute
1½ cups (355 ml) low-sodium chicken broth, defatted
4½ cups (1.1 l) spring water
1 cup (240 ml) wild rice

Equipment

1 large saucepan
wooden spoon

*Serve this with any meat dish
or plain beans*

94

10 minutes	Prepare ingredients as listed.
2 minutes	Spray saucepan liberally with olive oil spray. Sauté garlic, onion and chili pepper until soft.
1 minute	Add the brown rice and spicy seasoning salt substitute, mix well.
25 minutes	Add the chicken broth and water. Bring to a boil, reduce to a simmer, cover and cook for 20 minutes.
25 minutes	Add the wild rice, stir, cover and cook for another 25 minutes until the liquid is absorbed. Add more water for softer rice, if desired.

Approximate nutritional analysis per serving:
Calories 170, Protein 5 g, Carbohydrates 35 g, Fat 1 g,
Saturated Fat <1 g, Cholesterol 0 mg, Sodium 5 mg

This rice dish can be frozen for up to 6 months.

A great change from white rice!!

Black Bean Soup

Serves 8

Delicious served with warm tortillas or corn chips.

Ingredients

2 cups (480 ml) dry black beans (soaked overnight) or
    3 16-oz cans (480 g each) black beans
olive oil spray
1 medium onion, diced
5 cloves garlic, minced
2 small mild chili peppers, seeded and diced
3 cups (720 ml) spring water
1 28-oz (840 ml) can low-fat beef broth
¼ cup (60 ml) beer, optional
2 teaspoons (10 ml) dried cilantro
1 bay leaf
1 teaspoon (5 ml) chili powder
salt and pepper to taste
3 tablespoons (45 ml) low-fat sour cream
¼ cup (60 ml) red pepper, seeded and finely sliced

Equipment

cast-iron pot
large bowl
can opener
blender or mixer wand
knife
measuring cup and spoons

Pick out any pebbles from beans. In a large bowl, soak beans overnight, covered with water, or cover with boiling water and soak 2 hours. Drain.

10 minutes   Prepare ingredients as listed.

5 minutes   Over medium heat, spray the bottom of the pot with olive oil spray. Sauté the onions until translucent. Add the garlic and chili pepper and sauté for another minute to release the flavors.

2 hours   Add the beans, water, beef broth, beer, if desired, and spices. Bring to a boil, then reduce heat and simmer covered for 2 hours—45 minutes if canned beans are used.

5 minutes   Remove bay leaf and discard. Remove half of the soup and put it in a blender. Blend until smooth and return it to the pot.

30 minutes   Continue to simmer uncovered until soup is thick, 30 minutes or less.

Salt and pepper to taste.

Garnish each serving with 1½ teaspoons (8 ml) of low-fat sour cream and slices of red pepper.

Approximate nutritional analysis per serving:
Calories 198, Protein 13 g, Carbohydrates 35 g, Fat 1 g,
Saturated Fat <1 g, Cholesterol 2 mg, Sodium 9 mg

Black beans are a great source of protein and kids love them!

Grandma's Chicken Soup

Serves 8

Ingredients

5 pound (2.3 kg) chicken (kosher is best)
3 quarts (2.9 l) water
1 large onion, peeled
1 small bunch fresh parsley
3 sprigs fresh dill
3 stalks celery with tops
2 medium carrots
1 small turnip
5 cloves of garlic, peeled
1 tablespoon (15 ml) kosher salt
2 teaspoons (10 ml) white pepper

Equipment

large soup pot
medium soup pot
strainer
cheese cloth
large slotted spoon
large spoon
bowl

As kids we loved to eat the boiled chicken fresh out of the pot. You can use it for chicken salad and sandwiches, too!

5 minutes	Wash chicken, neck and innards with cold water and place in large soup pot.
2 minutes	Add all of the vegetables and spices to the pot.
	Pour in enough water to cover the chicken—3 quarts, more or less.
1½ hours	Bring to a boil, cover and reduce to a simmer. Simmer for 1½ hours.
10 minutes	Remove the chicken from the pot and put it in a large bowl. Remove all of the skin and return it to the soup. Debone the chicken meat and set aside in the refrigerator. Return the bones to the soup, including any broth that has accumulated in the bowl.
2 hours	Cover and simmer for 2 hours.
	Using the slotted spoon, remove the vegetables and bones from the soup and put in a bowl.
5 minutes	Line the strainer with a piece of cheesecloth (or paper towel) and place it over the medium soup pot. Pour the soup through the strainer into the pot.
1 minute	Discard the vegetables, skin and bone. Strain any broth that has accumulated in the bowl into the pot.
	Cover and let cool, then refrigerate overnight. (If you have a fat skimmer, you can drain off the fat and serve the same day. I always think the soup tastes better after a night in the refrigerator!)
	Skim any fat from the top of the pot with a spoon and discard. Reheat soup and serve.
	Add some chopped up chicken, thinly sliced carrots and celery, cooked noodles, cooked rice or matzoh balls.

Approximate nutritional analysis per 1 cup serving, skimmed of all fat:
Calories 65, Protein 2 g, Carbohydrates 10 g, Fat 2 g,
Saturated Fat <1 g, Cholesterol 0 mg, Sodium 592 mg

Mushroom-Barley Soup

Serves 6

Ingredients
olive oil spray
1 small white onion, diced
½ cup (120 ml) crimini mushrooms, sliced
½ cup (120 ml) oyster mushrooms, halved
½ cup (120 ml) portobello mushrooms cubed
½ cup (120 ml) regular mushrooms, minced,
    or 2 cups of any two or three varieties
4 cloves fresh garlic, minced
12-oz can (360 ml) beef broth, fat skimmed
1 cup (240 ml) spring water
1 jigger of dry sherry
salt and pepper to taste
1 cup (240 ml) barley

Equipment
knife
medium soup pot
can opener
measuring cup and spoons

You may substitute chicken broth for the beef broth if you like.

10 minutes	Prepare ingredients as listed.
3 minutes	Spray pot with olive oil spray. Over medium heat, sauté onions until translucent.
5 minutes	Add all the mushrooms and spray them with olive oil spray. Sauté until the juices start to be released. Add the garlic, stir. Continue cooking until mushrooms appear soft.
5 minutes	Add the beef broth, water and sherry. Bring to a boil.
30-40 minutes	Add the barley. Reduce heat and simmer until barley is soft. Salt and pepper to taste.

Approximate nutritional analysis per serving:
Calories 153, Protein 5 g, Carbohydrates 32 g, Fat <1 g,
Saturated Fat <1 g, Cholesterol 0 mg, Sodium 11 mg

This was my Uncle Ben's favorite soup.
It's heaven, so they must serve it there!

101

Potato-Leek Soup

Serves 8

Ingredients

butter-flavored oil spray
2 medium leeks, cleaned with much of the
    green removed, sliced
3 cloves garlic, sliced
3 cups (720 ml) chicken stock, defatted,
    canned or homemade
8 medium red potatoes, peeled and sliced
½ teaspoon (3 ml) white pepper
2 tablespoons (30 ml) dry sherry
1 cup (240 ml) low-fat milk
salt to taste
1 cup (240 ml) nonfat croutons
parsley flakes

Equipment

knife
medium soup pot
blender or blending wand
peeler
can opener
measuring cup and spoons

Serve this soup hot or cold.

102

30 minutes	Prepare ingredients as listed.
5 minutes	Spray pot liberally with buttered-flavored oil spray. Over medium heat, sauté leeks until translucent. Add garlic, sauté another minute, but do not allow garlic to burn.
35 minutes	Add chicken stock, potatoes and white pepper. Bring to a boil, then reduce heat, cover and simmer until potatoes are tender, about 30 minutes.
5 minutes	Using a blending wand directly in the pot, or transferring to a blender, blend soup until smooth. Add sherry, simmer for 5 more minutes to burn off the alcohol.
2 minutes	Slowly add milk, stirring continuously until well incorporated.

Serve garnished with nonfat croutons and parsley flakes.

Approximate nutritional analysis per serving:
Calories 116, Protein 3 g, Carbohydrates 23 g, Fat 1 g,
Saturated Fat <1 g, Cholesterol 1 mg, Sodium 54 mg

This freezes well, but don't add the milk until you are ready to serve.

Pumpkin-Lentil Soup

Serves 6-8

Ingredients

olive oil spray

1 medium onion, diced

3 cloves garlic, minced

2 cups (480 ml) chicken stock, defatted (canned
   or homemade)

16 oz (480 g) plain pumpkin purée or
   2 cups (480 ml) fresh pumpkin meat, diced

1 cup (240 ml) dried lentils

½ teaspoon (3 ml) dried marjoram

¼ teaspoon (1 ml) cumin

½ teaspoon (3 ml) thyme

½ teaspoon (3 ml) black pepper

1 cup (240 ml) evaporated nonfat milk

salt to taste

Equipment

medium pot

blender

knife

can opener

measuring cup and spoons

Very festive during the autumn holidays!

104

If you've got a pumpkin hanging around, scoop out the seeds, bake it at 350 degrees until tender, about 1 hour. Cool. Remove the flesh and dice.

10 minutes   Then prepare ingredients as listed.

5 minutes   Spray pot with olive oil spray. Over medium heat, sauté onions until translucent. Add the garlic and sauté another minute.

1½ hours   Add the chicken stock, pumpkin, lentils and spices. Bring to a boil then reduce heat and simmer for 1½ hours until lentils are soft.

5 minutes   Remove 1½ cups of mixture and put into a blender. Blend until smooth and return to pot.

15 minutes   Add evaporated nonfat milk and stir. Salt to taste. Simmer for 15 minutes.

Serve.

Approximate nutritional analysis per serving:
Calories 195, Protein 13 g, Carbohydrates 32 g, Fat 1.5 g,
Saturated Fat <1 g, Cholesterol 3 mg, Sodium 57 mg

Try this recipe with butternut squash instead. Golden and delicious!

Full of betacarotene!

Basic Béchamel

Yields 2½ cups (600 ml)

Prep
2 min
Cook
12 min

Ingredients

1 tablespoon (15 ml) low-fat margarine
2 tablespoons (30 ml) flour
12-oz can (360 ml) nonfat evaporated milk
1 cup (240 ml) low-fat milk
½ teaspoon (3 ml) salt
½ teaspoon (3 ml) white pepper
¼ teaspoon (1 ml) garlic powder
2 pinches nutmeg

Equipment

small saucepan
small bowl
whisk
measuring cup and spoons

Add a few squeezes of lemon juice for a great fish sauce.

2 minutes	Prepare ingredients as listed.
2 minutes	Blend the margarine and flour together with your fingers to make a roux. Set aside.
10 minutes	Combine evaporated milk, low-fat milk in a saucepan. Bring to a slow simmer over low heat, whisking continuously. Add the spices and stir until thick.
10 minutes	Whisking continuously, add a teaspoon of the roux at a time to the milk mixture, letting it dissolve before adding more. Continue to whisk as the sauce thickens. The longer it cooks, the thicker it gets.

Serve over pasta or chicken.

Approximate nutritional analysis per ⅛ cup serving:
Calories 11, Protein <1 g, Carbohydrates 1 g, Fat <1 g,
Saturated Fat <1 g, Cholesterol 1 mg, Sodium 39 mg

Add 1 teaspoon cornstarch to thicken even more.

Basic Tomato Sauce

Yields 5 cups (1.2 l)

Mommom Millie called this Tomato Gravy.

Ingredients

olive oil spray
5 cloves fresh garlic
2 32-oz cans (960 g each) crushed tomatoes
1 tablespoon (15 ml) dried oregano
1 tablespoon (15 ml) dried basil
2 tablespoons (30 ml) dried parsley
1 large bay leaf
1 teaspoon (5 ml) black pepper
salt to taste
2 teaspoons (10 ml) sugar, optional
¼ cup (60 ml) dry red wine
1 cup (240 ml) spring water
3 tablespoons (45 ml) Parmesan cheese, optional

Equipment

large soup pot
can opener
knife
measuring cups and spoons

Sugar cuts the acid of tomatoes.

Prep 18 min

Cook 2 hrs

108

5 minutes	Prepare ingredients as listed.
2 minutes	Warm pot over medium heat. Spray liberally with olive oil spray and sauté garlic; do not let it burn.
1 minute	Pour in tomatoes and add all of the spices. Add the sugar, if desired, wine and water and stir well.
10 minutes	Bring sauce to a boil, then reduce heat to a simmer
2 hours	Simmer two hours or until reduced by a third.
	Add Parmesan.
	Serve over pasta or chicken.

Approximate nutritional analysis per ½ cup serving:
Calories 47, Protein 2 g, Carbohydrates 9 g, Fat 1 g,
Saturated Fat <1 g, Cholesterol 0 mg, Sodium 296 mg

For a richer sauce, sauté a small can of tomato paste with the garlic before you add the rest of the ingredients.

This sauce freezes well.

Meat Sauce

Yields 2 quarts (1.9 l)

Ingredients

olive oil spray
1 lb (455 g) 90 percent lean ground beef
1 lb (455 g) 99 per cent lean white meat ground turkey
1 large white onion, diced
5 cloves fresh garlic, minced
6-oz can (180 g) tomato paste
2 32-oz cans (960 g each) crushed tomatoes
¼ cup (60 ml) fresh parsley, minced
2 large bay leaves
1 tablespoon (15 ml) dried oregano
2 cups (480 ml) spring water
¼ cup (60 ml) dry red wine

Equipment

large soup pot
can opener
strainer or colander
knife
fork
measuring cups and spoons

Substitute a variety of vegetables for the meat, such as mushrooms, peppers and carrots for a hearty vegetable sauce!

110

10 minutes	Prepare ingredients as listed.
12 minutes	Place pot over medium heat. Spray pot liberally with olive oil spray. Brown ground beef and turkey. Using a fork, break up meat into small bits cooking it until all the juice evaporates and only the meat and fat remain.
	Drain off the fat by pouring the meat into a colander set aside.
2 minutes	Sauté the onion in the pot until translucent; add the garlic, continue to sauté lightly (add more oil spray, if necessary). Do not let burn!
3 minutes	Add the tomato paste and cook, stirring continually until paste is steaming.
2 minutes	Add the canned tomatoes and blend until paste is incorporated.
1 minute	Return the meat to the pot and add all the spices, the wine and water.
2 hours	Bring to a boil then reduce heat. Simmer for 2 hours reducing by a third. Serve over pasta.

Approximate nutritional analysis per ½ cup serving:
Calories 168, Protein 17 g, Carbohydrates 9 g, Fat 2 g,
Saturated Fat <1 g, Cholesterol 11 mg, Sodium 264 mg

This sauce freezes well and makes lots!

You may use all turkey
instead of beef.

Perfect Puttanesca Sauce

Serves 6

Prep
12 min

Cook
40 min

Ingredients

5 cloves garlic, minced
olive oil spray
32-oz can (960 g) crushed tomatoes
¼ teaspoon (1 ml) dried red pepper
1 teaspoon (5 ml) dried oregano
1 tablespoon (15 ml) dried parsley
6 black cured olives, pitted and diced
1 tablespoon (15 ml) capers, rinsed
1 can flat anchovy filets, rinsed and minced finely

Equipment

medium saucepan
knife
measuring spoons

I adore this sauce as spicy as I can get it so I add more red pepper.

112

10 minutes	Prepare all ingredients as listed.
1 minute	Over medium heat, sauté the garlic in olive oil spray. Do not let the garlic burn.
1 minute	Add the crushed tomatoes, spices, olives, and anchovies.
30 minutes	Bring to a boil and then reduce to a simmer. Simmer for 30 minutes.
10 minutes	Add the capers and cook for 10 minutes more.
	Serve over pasta.

Approximate nutritional analysis per serving:
Calories 56, Protein 4 g, Carbohydrates 8 g, Fat 2 g,
Saturated Fat <1 g, Cholesterol 6 mg, Sodium 673 mg

Try this sauce over ziti or rigatoni.

White Clam Sauce

Serves 6

Ingredients

2 cup (480 ml) spring water
6 cloves garlic, 3 minced, 3 whole
1 bay leaf
3 dozen small little neck clams or 1½ dozen large clams
olive oil spray
1 small white onion, diced
¼ cup (60 ml) dry white wine
1 teaspoon (5 ml) oregano
6 fresh medium basil leaves, chopped
½ teaspoon (3 ml) salt
½ teaspoon (3 ml) pepper
6 plum tomatoes, seeded and chopped
1 lb (455 g) linguini, cooked and drained

Equipment

medium saucepan
steamer
large frying pan
strainer
cheese cloth or paper towel
2 medium bowls
knife
measuring cup and spoons

If you choose to use canned clams include a bottle of clam juice and add the clam after you sauté the onions and garlic.

114

5 minutes	Prepare ingredients as listed.
	In a medium saucepan, place the water, whole garlic and bay leaf. Insert the steamer.
5 minutes	Scrub the clams under cold water. Discard any that open.
12 minutes	Put clams in pot, cover and bring the water to a boil. Reduce heat to medium and steam clams until they open. Discard any clams that do not open.
1 minute	Remove the clams and set aside.
1 minute	Pour the water in which the clams were steamed through a strainer lined with a piece of cheese cloth into a bowl. Set aside.
5 minutes	In a large frying pan, over medium heat, sauté the onion in olive oil spray until translucent. Add the garlic slices and continue sautéing for another minute.
7 minutes	Add the strained clam juice, the wine and spices. Raise the heat and bring to a boil for 5 minutes to burn off the alcohol and reduce. Add the chopped tomatoes and return the clams in their shells to the sauce. Mix well and cook for another 2 minutes.
	At this point add your cooked pasta to the pan and toss for a minute or two. Serve immediately.

Approximate nutritional analysis per serving:
Calories 342, Protein 15 g, Carbohydrates 60 g, Fat 3 g,
Saturated Fat <1 g, Cholesterol 12.5 mg, Sodium 205 mg

For red clam sauce use basic tomato sauce or fresh tomato sauce recipe, throw in cleaned clams, shell and all. Put a lid on and let cook until clams open.

Carrot Cake with Icing

Serves 10

My friend Jimmy thinks this is the best he's tasted!

Ingredients

2¼ cups (540 ml) sifted unbleached white flour
1 teaspoon (5 ml) baking soda
1 teaspoon (5 ml) baking powder
½ teaspoon (3 ml) salt
½ cup (8 tablespoons) (120 ml) extra low-fat margarine
1 cup (240 ml) raw or blonde sugar
½ cup (120 ml) egg substitute
1 teaspoon (5 ml) vanilla extract
1 teaspoon (5 ml) nutmeg
½ teaspoon (3 ml) cinnamon
1 cup (240 ml) low-fat buttermilk
⅓ cup (80 ml) 1 percent milk
2 cups (480 ml) carrot, shredded
1 cup (240 ml) raisins
butter-flavored oil spray

1 tablespoon (15 ml) flour

Icing

8 oz (240 g) Neufchâtel cream cheese
8 oz (240 g) fat-free cream cheese
½ cup (120 ml) confectioners sugar
¼ cup (60 ml) honey

Equipment

large bowl
2 medium bowls
measuring cups and spoons
hand mixer
food processor or hand grater
sifter
2 9-inch cake pans

Bake the batter in muffin tins for quick snacks. Ice them for cupcakes.

116

Preheat oven to 350 degrees (180°C).

10 minutes   Prepare ingredients as listed.

2 minutes   Sift the flour, then resift together with the baking soda, baking powder and salt into a medium bowl.

3 minutes   In a large bowl, beat the margarine, sugar, egg substitute, vanilla and spices until smooth.

1 minute   Combine the buttermilk and low-fat milk. Set aside.

5 minutes   Add ⅓ of the flour mixture to the sugar mixture and begin to blend. Add ⅓ of the liquid mixture and continue in thirds until all ingredients are incorporated, and you have a smooth batter.

1 minute   Add the carrots and raisins and mix well.

5 minutes   Spray the cake pans with butter spray and lightly flour.

2 minutes   Pour the batter evenly into the cake pans and spread smooth to the edges.

Bake at 350 degrees (180°C) for 40 minutes or until a toothpick inserted near the center comes out clean.

5 minutes   Make the Icing while the cake is cooling by combining all ingredients into a bowl and blending with the hand mixer until smooth and creamy.

Ice the cake when completely cool.

Refrigerate until serving time or freeze.

Approximate nutritional analysis per serving:
Calories 498, Protein 12 g, Carbohydrates 79 g, Fat 9 g,
Saturated Fat 5 g, Cholesterol 25 mg, Sodium 572 mg

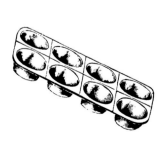

Chocolate Buttermilk Cake

Serves 10

Ingredients

butter-flavored oil spray

2 cups (480 ml) sifted unbleached all-purpose flour,
    plus 2 tablespoons (30 ml)

1 teaspoon (5 ml) baking soda

¼ teaspoon (1 ml) salt

½ cup (120 ml) extra low-fat margarine

1 cup (240 ml) sugar

¼ cup (60 ml) egg substitute

1½ teaspoons (8 ml) vanilla

¾ cup (240 ml) unsweetened cocoa powder,
    plus 1 teaspoon

1 cup (240 ml) low-fat buttermilk

⅓ cup (80 ml) 1 percent milk

Icing

1 cup (240 ml) confectioners sugar, plus 1 teaspoon (5 ml)

1½ oz (45 g) melted unsweetened chocolate

4 oz (120 g) Neufchâtel cream cheese

½ cup (120 ml) nonfat sour cream

Equipment

3 medium bowls

hand mixer

sifter

measuring cup and spoons

spatula

spoon

2 9-inch round cake pans

Enjoy!

118

Preheat oven to 350 degrees (180°C).

10 minutes Prepare ingredients for cake as listed.

5 minutes Spray cake pans with butter flavored spray. Dust with 2 tablespoons of flour. Discard extra. Set pans aside.

2 minutes Sift flour, then resift with baking soda and salt. Set aside in medium bowl.

5 minutes Combine margarine, sugar, egg substitute, vanilla and all but 1 teaspoon of cocoa powder. Blend with hand mixer until smooth.

2 minutes Add buttermilk and milk, beat until well blended.

3 minutes Add the dry ingredients to the liquid mixture slowly as you continue to blend.

1 minute Pour half in each pan and smooth with a spatula.

30 minutes Bake for 30 minutes or until a toothpick inserted near the center comes out clean.

5 minutes While cake is baking, make the Icing. Combine all but 1 teaspoon of confectioners sugar with the Neufchâtel cream cheese and nonfat sour cream. Put in the refrigerator to chill for 30 minutes.

30 minutes Let the cake cool.

10 minutes Take the icing out of the refrigerator about 10 minutes before frosting the cake. Ice when cake is cooled by spreading the icing evenly on the top of one layer. Place the other layer on top and frost top and sides.

2 minutes Sprinkle the top with the remaining teaspoon of cocoa powder and confectioners sugar.

Approximate nutritional analysis per serving:
Calories 320, Protein 9 g, Carbohydrates 68 g, Fat 7 g,
Saturated Fat 3 g, Cholesterol 10 mg, Sodium 328 mg

Flan

Serves 8

Ingredients

½ cup (120 ml) white sugar
14-oz can (420 ml) sweetened nonfat condensed milk
3 large eggs
1 teaspoon (5 ml) pure vanilla
3 cups (720 ml) 1 percent milk

Equipment

medium baking dish or 8 6-oz ramekins
small saucepan
whisk
large baking pan
large mixing bowl
measuring cups and spoons

Try orange or almond extract instead of vanilla for a different taste.

Preheat oven to 400 degrees (205°C).

30 minutes In a small saucepan over high heat, caramelize the white sugar. Pour the melted sugar into the medium baking dish or divide among the ramekins and set aside to cool.

3 minutes Combine the condensed milk, eggs, vanilla and milk. Whisk until well blended. Pour the liquid into the baking dish or ramekins.

1 hour Fill the large baking pan with 1 inch of water and place in the oven. Carefully place the medium baking dish or ramekins into the water bath. Bake at 400 degrees (205°C) for 45 minutes to 1 hour until firm.

Let cool then refrigerate for 12 hours for best flavor.

Approximate nutritional analysis per serving:
Calories 272, Protein 10 g, Carbohydrates 44 g, Fat 3 g,
Saturated Fat 1.5 g, Cholesterol 104 mg, Sodium 138 mg

For flan with 1 gram of fat and less cholesterol, use egg substitute instead of real eggs.

Lemon Cheesecake

10 servings

Ingredients

16 oz (480 g) fat-free cream cheese
8 oz (240 g) light cream cheese
1 cup (240 ml) nonfat sour cream
½ cup (120 ml) egg substitute
1 cup (240 ml) sugar
1 teaspoon (5 ml) vanilla
juice of half a lemon
½ teaspoon (3 ml) lemon rind
2 egg whites
½ teaspoon (3 ml) salt
oil spray
1 tablespoon (15 ml) flour

Equipment

12-inch springform pan
large bowl
small bowl
hand mixer
measuring cup and spoons

Instead of lemon, add almond extract or 1/2 cup (120 ml) cocoa powder for chocolate cheesecake.

122

Preheat oven to 350 degrees (180°C).

5 minutes Prepare ingredients as listed.

5 minutes In the large bowl, blend together cream cheese, sour cream, egg substitute, sugar, vanilla, lemon juice and lemon rind until creamy smooth.

5 minutes In the small bowl, whip egg whites with salt until firm but not stiff.

1 minute Fold the egg whites into the batter until incorporated.

1 minute Spray the springform pan with oil spray and coat with flour. Shake off excess.

1 hour 20 minutes Bake for 1 hour 20 minutes or until center is firm.

Serve garnished with fresh fruit.

Approximate nutritional analysis per serving:
Calories 332, Protein 8 g, Carbohydrates 24 g, Fat 5 g,
Saturated Fat 2 g, Cholesterol 48 mg, Sodium 353 mg

You can make this cake with all cream cheese, substituting 8 ounces light cream cheese for the sour cream.

Sour Apple Pie

Serves 10

Ingredients

Filling:

3 lbs (1.4 kg) Granny Smith apples, cored, peeled and sliced

1 teaspoon (5 ml) cinnamon

1 teaspoon (5 ml) nutmeg

¼ teaspoon (1 ml) mace

¼ cup (60 ml) honey

juice of 1 lemon

3 tablespoons (45 ml) unbleached white flour

Double Crust

2¼ cups (540 ml) unbleached white flour

1 teaspoon (5 ml) salt

2 teaspoon (10 ml) sugar

½ cup (120 ml) extra low–fat margarine, cold

8 tablespoons (120 ml) ice water (approximately)

Equipment

pie plate

rolling pin

large bowl

small bowl

peeler

juicer dish

food processor

measuring cup and spoons

fork

Serve this warm with light whipped cream topping or low-fat vanilla ice milk.

124

3 minutes	To make Crust, sift together flour, salt and sugar.
3 minutes	Put margarine in a food processor. Pour in flour mixture and blend together. Add the ice water a tablespoon at a time until dough begins to hold together.
2 minutes	Test dough by pinching it between your fingers. If it holds together moistly it is ready. If not, add another tablespoon of water. On a floured work surface, knead it into a ball. Cut in half and make two balls. Cover with wax paper and set aside.
5 minutes	To prepare Filling, mix together apple slices, spices, honey, lemon juice and flour in a large bowl. Mix until apples are well coated.
	Flour your rolling pin and work surface. Roll out one dough ball to extend 2 inches beyond the edge of the pie plate.
	Lay dough into the pie plate, roll edges up and press them down with your thumb.
12 minutes	Roll the other dough to the same size. Fold in half and set aside.
5 minutes	Fill the pie plate with apple mixture and pat down.
3 minutes	Unfold the other dough onto the top of the apples and press edges into bottom dough securely. Poke holes in the top dough with a fork.
1 hour 15 minutes	Bake at 350 degrees (180°C) for 1 hour 15 minutes or until crust is lightly browned.

Approximate nutritional analysis per serving:
Calories 318, Protein 3.5 g, Carbohydrates 59 g, Fat 5 g,
Saturated Fat 1 g, Cholesterol 0 mg, Sodium 382 mg

The original recipe, made by a friend of my parents, used lots of butter and the juice of 6 lemons. Only for the bravest taste buds!

Index

Coming soon . . .

My Grandmother's Table
Volume II

We would love to hear from you about these recipes,
and low-fat cooking ideas of your own.

Write to
Gardner Publishing
"My Grandmother's Table"
PO Box 3017TCB
West Orange, NJ 07052